CRITICAL ACCLAIM FOR
DON'T SHOOT THE DRUMMER

"With its hard-hitting prose and smooth groove, Jonathan Brown's *Don't Shoot the Drummer* is tight, man. It goes down like a chilled bourbon after a long day of Crashing."
—Tim O'Mara, author of the
Raymond Donne series
and editor of *Down to the River*

"Lou Crasher is back! In a virtuoso performance, *Don't Shoot the Drummer* pulses with relentless action and heart as Crasher rolls through the streets of L.A. in search of the killer (or killers) of a popular student and football player. A modern-day Archer or Spenser, Crasher puts it all on the line to get to the truth, and deliver justice to those the system has left behind."
—Shawn Reilly Simmons, author of the
Red Carpet Catering Mysteries

"Come for the extraordinary characters, stay for the kick-ass fights; come for the back-stage rock scene, stay for the sandwiches; come for the voice, stay for the coolest set of images this side of the wise-cracking heroes of '30's movies. Whatever brings you into Lou Crasher's world, you'll be glad you came."
—SJ Rozan, bestselling author of *Paper Son*

DON'T SHOOT
THE DRUMMER

OTHER TITLES BY
JONATHAN J. BROWN

The Lou Crasher Thrillers
The Big Crescendo
Don't Shoot the Drummer
Drums, Guns N Money

The Doug "Moose" McCrae Thrillers
Moose's Law

Other Titles

A Boxing Trainer's Journey:
A Novel Based on the Life of Angelo Dundee

JONATHAN J. BROWN

DON'T SHOOT THE DRUMMER

A LOU CRASHER THRILLER

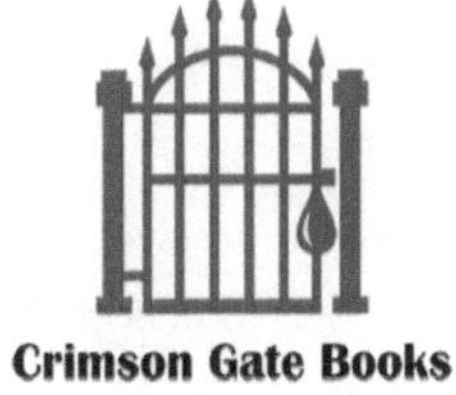

Crimson Gate Books

To those who put the needs of others
before their own...*the selfless.*

PROLOGUE

A half-dozen names bounced around between the L.A.P.D. and the media until somewhere along the way the "tent gang" stuck. It was the label Los Angelinos settled on when referring to the band of thieves that burgled unoccupied homes tented off for fumigation. The crew consisted of only three members. In the past two and a half months they'd robbed eight homes, all in upscale neighborhoods, in a seemingly random pattern that left the police completely ineffective. The crew rarely used phones but when they did, they were always prepaid burner phones, which they never purchased at the same place twice. They texted in code when necessary and only referred to one another with nicknames, all of which were alcoholic drinks. They were Moscow Mule, the unofficial ringleader, Boilermaker and I.P.A.— the abbreviated term for India Pale Ale beer.

On Friday, August thirteenth, at four a.m., they'd sliced a tent, even though they could have easily unsnapped the clips, popped the back door-slider and killed the alarm in forty-two seconds. They each took to their knees and drank in the quiet for fifteen seconds. It wouldn't make sense for someone to be inside a tented home; still, they took precautions. Silently they rose as a unit and made their way to their designated section of the home. It was always the same: hit your territory, clean it, then meet back at the entry point in eleven minutes and fifty-nine seconds or less. Each member was agile, had nerves of Kevlar and, above all, was loyal to the group.

Moscow was eight minutes deep and in the upstairs master bedroom when a presence was felt. The muzzle of a Glock 17 to the back of the skull confirmed this suspicion.

"Drop that shit and come with me. You fucks ain't makin' ten houses. Shit, you ain't makin' nine. Move!"

Moscow knew it wasn't the cops. They'd have identified themselves as L.A.P.D. or Sheriff's whatever. The lone gunman marched Moscow down the stairs to the kitchen where the ringleader saw Boilermaker and I.P.A. bound and gagged with duct tape. They squirmed and growled when they saw Moscow. The gunman shoved Moscow alongside the others and applied the tape.

Fucking "rent-a-cop," Moscow thought, reading the man's private neighborhood security uniform and nametag. Moscow put Billups at twenty, twenty-two years old, tops—a novice probably thinking he'd be a hero.

"Well look at this," Billups said, puffing out his chest. "I never thought I'd—"

But that was as far as he got. Two closely grouped *pfft* sounds came from the dark hallway behind the security guard. The first shot took his right ear off. The kill shot splattered his right cheek, eye and a mini portion of his jaw against the wall behind him. His body spun one-hundred-and-eighty degrees, smashed hard into the wall, and slowly slid down to the floor. His left eye was wide in a what-the-fuck-just-happened expression. Hurried footsteps retreated down the hall. A door slammed, then all was quiet. Moscow was the first to react by inching toward the kitchen island, overturning a wooden block of knives, and manipulate one to cut the duct tape loose. The ringleader wasted no time freeing the others.

"What in the fuck, Moscow? Who in the—"

"Doesn't matter. We're out. Grab that bag and let's blow."

"But my shit is still—"

"Wanna explain it to the cops? Get your shit together, Boiler."

While Boilermaker and Moscow argued, I.P.A. sprayed a quick note on the massive subzero tent in spray paint.

"Let's go I.P.A., fuck," Moscow barked.

"Never without the signature, suckaz."

Moscow grabbed the bag and glanced at I.P.A.'s handy work on the way out. It was slightly different each time. This particular message was shorter due to the circumstances. The press will love pixelating this one, Moscow thought.

Ya been cock fucked. The Tent Gang!

CHAPTER ONE

I opened the screen door and walked into Ida's old-school diner, which was nestled between a low-rise apartment building and a tiny laundromat in west Studio City. Ida's clientele loved her. Although she was technically not a chef, her clientele would beg to differ. Her menu was simple: mixed down-home southern with local Mexican flavor and something else no one could put their finger on. Ida's was my favorite breakfast and lunch diner in L.A. It also happened to be my half-brother Jake's fave spot as well. It's scary how much the two of us have in common.

A quick sweep of the place revealed the usual gathering of customers, but it was the two hard men in trench coats that troubled me. As I strolled down the breakfast bar I nodded to a few regulars, even patted Simon, the slope-shouldered shoe-repair guy on the back—good dude. Mid-stroll along the long faux granite countertop, I slid onto a red leather-cushioned stool beside a Filipina woman in a bus driver's uniform. We exchanged a brief hello before I called to Ida, whose back was to me.

"Afternoon Ida," I said.

She turned with a grin she shares with the world on the daily, "Lou, how are things outside my door?" she said and filled my coffee mug.

"It's all rock 'n' roll to me, baby," I said, feigning a casual manner.

Ida forced a laugh. Her hand shook slightly as she moved from my cup to the female bus driver's.

"How's business?" I asked.

"Business is good," she said, moving a few strands of hair that had escaped her pony- tail and were partially blocking her vision. "Because this girl," she said, pointing a thumb at herself, "knows what she's doing." Her face reddened slightly—nerves.

The bus driver raised her cup in agreement. I smiled briefly before grabbing a napkin and scribbling upside down on it.

'Two trench coats. Booth 3, the assholes you told me about?'

Ida grabbed a rag and wiped the area around my table setting. Barely moving her lips, she whispered, "Don't know 'em, don't like the look."

"Okay. Relax," I whispered back.

The rag got tossed onto the counter behind her before she eased down the breakfast bar. I picked up the front section of a discarded newspaper and skimmed the headlines while using the overhead mirror to glance at the two trench-coated patrons. The huge headline at the top of the front page shouted, "Tent gang kills security guard in ninth burglary." During the past couple of months, this so-called "tent gang" had been hitting homes that had been tented for fumigation, but this was the first time they'd killed someone. I glanced back up at the trench coats in the overhead mirror, whose booth was halfway between the side entrance and the restrooms. They were both thickset with patchy beards. More than likely they were carrying—hence the coats. Their body language was tense and had grown more so as they watched the dialog between Ida and me. This felt like a robbery was imminent, like when famed racehorse Secretariat was out front by three lengths coming into the final stretch in the Kentucky Derby.

A man in his mid-seventies wearing a plain green golf shirt tucked into high-waisted Toughskins slid onto the stool next to me. His mustache was snow-white and thicker than film actor Sam Elliott's. His close-cropped hair was eighty percent salt, twenty percent black peppercorn. There was no slouch to his posture and his chest and arms were impressive for his age. I knew at a glance that he was not only fit, he was capable.

"Afternoon friend. Name's Prescott Johanssen. Guys in my unit called me Press."

"Vietnam?" I turned slightly and shook the man's hand. Prescott winked.

"Lou Crasher."

Prescott leaned across me as if reaching for the sugar and lowered his voice.

"I notice you've clocked the two trench coat assholes. I'm old but I'm ready. You lead. I'll back you up. I'm not heeled but I do have Betsy."

I raised my eyebrows.

"My five-inch Browning Russ Kommer blade. And by the way," he said, dumping a healthy portion of sugar into his coffee cup, "I'm also a retired state trooper."

Capable.

I took another peek at the two men. They couldn't hide the angst from their thick builds, which suggested the mission was a "go." I nodded to Prescott and moved with purpose. All patrons' eyes tracked me. A brunette in her early twenties stopped chatting with her boyfriend and began filming with her cell phone. I stopped at the booth, put both hands on the tabletop, and leaned forward.

"Get up, get out and never come back," I said.

"Piss off. It's a free country…brutha."

"This part ain't and it's expensive."

The man to my left had a heavy forehead that looked as though several knuckles had been busted on it. He tried an upward punch from where he sat while attempting to stand. I leaned my head back, avoiding the shot, while simultaneously giving a short punch to the nose of the guy to my right. The shot bloodied his nose and knocked him against the corner of the booth. Forehead recoiled and managed to get a Ruger P95 handgun out of his coat. He swung it, right-handed, aiming at my face. I grabbed the arm by the wrist and slammed it hard on the table twice. The gun dropped to the floor. I kicked it behind me toward Prescott—I hoped. A patron screamed. I gave the gunman a quick palm strike to the nose before pivoting back to Nosebleed.

Nosebleed managed to get out of the booth and launch a left cross, catching me on the jaw. I rolled with it, softening the blow, and grabbed him by the wrist of his left hand. I gave him a short chop to the windpipe with the edge of my right hand. He choked and clutched at his throat. I didn't give him a chance to recover. Holding the wrist, I moved in an almost dance maneuver under the man's arm and yanked hard, pulling him over my back. It was a classic judo flip. The man landed hard, the back of his skull connecting brutally with the tile floor, knocking him semi-conscious.

The other man leapt out of the booth and hoofed it toward the gun, shoving a small Latina woman out of her chair as he barreled by. Somebody by the front door screamed at the fracas. As the big man neared the gun, I realized I had wasted too much time on his partner. Heavy Forehead bent to retrieve the Ruger.

But I had a one-man cavalry. Prescott stood in a wide bowler's stance. He was a south-paw, which meant he held the three-quarters-full glass coffee pot in his left hand. With knees slightly bent he swung the pot backward then accelerated a looping underhand strike. The pot shattered, enveloping the man's face and torso in glass and hot coffee. He fell to the floor and rolled around screaming. Prescott stood over the man with a sneer on his face. The black pot handle shook in his liver-spotted hand. His right eye twitched slightly.

"Stow it, scumbag, before I really give you something to cry about," Prescott said, giving him a swift kick in his ribs. "Kids today...goddamn disgrace."

I fell in behind my ally and thanked him while simultaneously taking what was left of the pot handle from him. A wail ripped through the restaurant, coming from the entrance. Heavy Forehead's bloody-nosed partner was three feet from us, moving fast, when he was stopped in his tracks and hauled backward. A muscled black man in jeans and a tight black T-shirt held the man by his collar and drove a solid knee into the small of his back.

As Nosebleed struggled to keep his feet, the brother took the opportunity to put his free hand around the man's throat and rapidly slam his head twice on a tabletop. Nosebleed went unconscious, but the Good Samaritan slammed him a third time, breaking off a triangular chunk of table, then let him drop to the floor without giving him so much as a glance. A quiet fell over the restaurant before applause broke out.

"Prescott Johanssen," I said. "Meet my brother, Jake."

CHAPTER TWO

The meeting Jake and I had arranged at Ida's was for him to hand over another yoga video. He was always complaining of my lack of flexibility when we trained together. He also claimed the type of breathing used in yoga would aid me in remaining calm in the heat of battle. As it turned out, Jake also had another reason for wanting to meet me: he needed my help—a first in our relationship. As soon as we got outside the diner, he had me haul out my phone and enter a name into my contacts.

"Okay, done. Who's Meredith Billups?" I asked.

"Mother of the security guard the tent gang canceled. And," he paused, "a friend. Call her. Help her."

And that was all he said before climbing onto his Ducati motorcycle. I headed to my ride as the cops entered the far end of the parking lot. Prescott Johanssen had said he'd handle them for us since Jake thought he and I shouldn't hang around.

I fired up the ol' gal, my 1965 Mustang, headed south on the 101 Freeway, and eased into Hollywood. With the bulk of the morning commuters out of the way I was able to hold steady at seventy miles an hour, my ride's favorite speed. After circling down the Cahuenga off-ramp the surface streets took me to the L.A. Practice Joint, my place of business.

The Practice Joint was a business set up for bands to rehearse. I'd been there just under two years, and although the pay wasn't great I got a kick out of the owner, Big Eddie Carruthers. He had his son Michael manage the place, a nice enough guy who meant well but wasn't really a strong leader. Big Eddie was the main reason I kept the job, but the other perk was the connections. Up to thirty bands came through each week and over time I'd parlayed that into more than a handful of decent gigs. Drummers flake, quit, get road gigs and fall prey to drugs all the time, and sometimes yours truly is in the center of the bull's eye, ready to save the drowning band.

I unlocked the security gate and opened the inner door. The pungent aroma of the previous night's marijuana, stale beer and sweat crawled up my nostrils. I walked down the dark, narrow hallway to the keypad and shut off the alarm. Entering the office, I grabbed the phone on the third ring.

"L.A. Practice Joint, this is Lou."

"Lou, ma boy. Eddie Carruthers, d'ya just get in?"

"Seconds ago, Big Eddie, how are ya?"

"Still with the Big Eddie stuff, huh?" he chuckled.

He once told me his football teammates called him that and that it was nice to hear it again.

"Listen, are ya in the mood for a promotion?" I could see his heavy jowl of a smile through the phone. His glasses would be dangling from the silver daisy chain since he'd just dialed a phone number. And even though he and his wife kept their apartment toasty warm, he'd be in his favorite light-brown cardigan.

"Promotions and cold beers are always welcome, sir."

"Heh, heh, my son has decided, yet again, to take his life down a different path. He's going back to school—he says," he paused to clear his throat. "Funny, in my day we went to school once then got on with it, that is, if we didn't get pulled into war."

"It's a different time," I said, which seemed an appropriate statement.

"Indeed. Anyway, I'd like to make you manager, how's that sound?"

"Sounds like a Dizzy Gillespie track. Will an increase in pay come with this amazing new title?"

"On to the numbers, I like that, Lou. How's fourteen bucks an hour?"

"I'd prefer twenty."

"Not a penny more than sixteen and I'm firm on that."

"You've got yourself a deal. And thanks, Big Eddie. I appreciate it. Hello Evie," I said, hearing his wife's quiet breathing on the other line.

"Congratulations Lou," she said. I could picture her smiling crow's feet at the corners of her gray eyes.

"Evie, you on the other phone? I warned you about that," Eddie barked.

"Oh, hush up, you; what do you think we have two lines for?"

"Well it sure isn't for—"

"Okay you two," I said as referee. "Thank you both for the promotion but, if you don't mind, I've got managerial duties to attend to."

They got a kick out of that, thanked me, then continued their squabble as they hung up. I put the smart phone back on the desk and left it off the charging/music doc with a smile. This day was looking up.

CHAPTER THREE

Meredith Billups lived in East Hollywood next to Barnsdell Art Park, about a ten-minute drive from the Practice Joint, barring traffic, but there was always traffic, so I'd be looking at fifteen to twenty minutes. The neighborhood around the park is a middle-class 'hood with most of the homes built in the early 1950s. Two bedrooms, one bath, on a three-thousand-foot lot seemed to be the standard. Modern apartment buildings were popping up at a quick rate with rent starting at twenty-two hundred dollars a month and steadily moving north.

Meredith's small home was pale blue with white trim and white rain gutters. The paint job was no more than three years old and her tiny front yard was uncluttered and nicely groomed. As I entered through the thigh-high gate, a crow took flight, landed on the roof's peak, and protested my visit.

After I was admitted, I considered using the flashlight on my cell phone to aid me down the home's dark entry hall. It was like spelunking as we negotiated the tight passage to her living room. The house smelled of cinnamon and sugar. My guess was cinnamon buns.

"Come on through, Mr. Crasher."

"Right behind you and, please, call me Lou."

Once in the bright, naturally lit living room I shook her bony hand, which had the long fingers of a pianist. Asparagus green was Meredith's favorite color and her son Cody had been her *everything* because he looked at me from every wall, window ledge, mantle, coffee table, and shelf. The place was a shrine to him. There were pictures both framed and loose, and a few on her walls had been blown up to poster-size.

I was guided to a large plush sofa with a dark green slipcover and thick, clear plastic protective cover—old school. In front of the sofa was a four-foot fiberboard coffee table. On top of a Sports Illustrated magazine sat two loose five-by-seven photos of Cody. The protective plastic snapped and popped as I sat down.

"Tea, Mr. Crash—um Lou? I'm having cinnamon chai."

"Yes, please. It smells great."

We blew on the tops of our mugs as we regarded each other.

"I can't begin to tell you how sorry I am for your loss, Ms. Billups."

Her "thank you" was barely above a whisper.

"Jake, my half-brother—not sure if you knew that—tells me you need my help. It's why I'm here today," I said.

"As you said on the phone," she sipped. "Got any credentials?"

"Officially no, but I've located a few things, including people, in my past. I can handle myself; I'm incorruptible but, best of all, Jake vouches for me."

Her dark brown eyes were a quarter shade shy of black, set far apart on her face and dipped down slightly at the corners. They'd been tearful for hours and had seen very little sleep. I felt for her. She seemed scarcely aware of the tea she slurped.

"I suppose I'm satisfied for now," she said finally.

"Tell me what you need, Ms. Billups."

"Need? I need my boy sitting in that spot instead of some stranger, that's what I need," she said, her voice raised slightly. With a shaky hand she put her teacup down on a doily coaster. I got up and moved to an antique hutch smothered in Cody photos.

"May I?" I asked, indicating an eight-by-ten in a gaudy gold frame. The grieving mother gave me a short nod. I looked at the photo of Cody in football gear on bended knee. I'd had several like it taken of of me in the past. Cody had penetrating football-player's eyes. Eyes that said he'd do anything his coach told him, no matter the damage to his body, so long as his team won the game. I'd been there. The game can do that to you. I turned to his mother.

"His size and the way he's gripping that football, I'd say he was a running back, yes?"

"*Starting* running back, Lou, every year he played."

"Then he was tough," I said. "We called his type studs."

"He most certainly was," her head nodded up and down several times. "You played?"

"A lifetime ago. Free safety," I said.

"Seek and destroy," she said with her lip curling up to the side.

"You know your football," I said. The lip curl became a weak smile. "If a guy like Cody busted through the line and beat the linebackers, I was the last line of defense."

"My boy'd have run over you like an eighteen-wheeler blasting through a shopping cart, Mr. Crasher," she said, eyeing me head to toe. "No offense."

"None taken," I said, knowing better than to dispute her claim. An awkward silence filled the space between us.

"Okay," she said finally. "Put that photo down, come look me in my eye and tell me you'll catch these tent muthafuckas that kilt my boy!"

I sat back down. "I don't work with cops. They'll work the case from their end, and I'll work from mine. That'll put the squeeze on the tent gang. I work mostly alone but Jake will lend a hand where needed. I'm confident we'll bring them to just—"

"S'pose you catch 'em but say, they corner you—back you against the wall," she paused, her eyes turning to slits. "Will you kill 'em?"

"I value my life above all else, so if they don't come quietly—" I let it hang. It was a bigger boast than planned. I was beginning to sound more like Jake than myself. It was probably because I wanted to come through for this woman, and Cody and Jake as well.

"That'll do for now, I s'pose." She rose from her seat. "Do you need anything from me before I go lie down?"

I told her I'd need phone numbers from Cody's best buds, cousins or girlfriends. She told me I'd have it all by the following day.

"That it?"

"Almost. Is Cody's father—"

"Dead and gone. Long ago," she said with eyes darkening. "And him I don't miss."

"Siblings?"

"Older brother, Darius, kilt in Iraq, 2016." She emphasized hard on the 'I' in Iraq. Tears filled her tired eyes. I wondered where the pictures of her other fallen son were.

"Shit," I whispered.

"Ol' Meredith Billups ain't got shit left, Lou, so bring these muthafuckas to justice, like you was gonna say earlier, and then and only then I'll have something." She looked down at the thick green carpet. "Then...I'll have something," she mumbled again, hauling what looked like aching bones out of her chair.

I swallowed hard, "Yes ma'am."

CHAPTER FOUR

Julie McCall, also known as the Trusty Lesbo, sat in her rented condo with the lights low. Her feet rested on her inner thighs in the classic yogic flying lotus position. A hot Mount Gay rum and water with a pinch of nutmeg steamed from the coffee mug at her elbow. Her hair, still wet from the shower, cooled her naked back. She heard the ping notification on her laptop. She opened it and saw Moscow Mule, although Moscow was oblivious that Trusty was watching. She had easily hacked Moscow's computer so that she could secretly observe everything through the laptop's camera lens. Trusty was the tent gang's quarterback. As their hacker, she was the one who regularly broke into fumigation companies' computers and scooped their work schedules. She also could manipulate any alarm systems in the homes they targeted. It was child's play for her.

She opened a tiny window on her laptop to spy what Moscow was checking: emails. Trusty checked the time: five p.m. The other tent crewmembers would have slept off the previous night's robbery and would be arriving at Moscow's any minute. They always gathered at Moscow's for a post-burglary powwow, which was why Trusty had set her own computer to alert her whenever Moscow's laptop was fired up. If Moscow left the computer off, there was always ALEXA, and failing that, there was the twenty-four-cubic-foot Samsung Smart fridge, all easy hacks for the Trusty Lesbo.

Moscow's door buzzer buzzed.

"*It's open,*" Moscow called, stepping away from the computer. Trusty reverse engineered the laptop's audio system and was also able to listen in on the group. They hugged it out at the door, grabbed drinks, then sat around Moscow's living room. Trusty grinned as she picked up the tension in the room. Moscow, the unofficial gang leader, took the floor.

"*Okay, look, last night was fucked, super fucked and—*"

"*It was that Trusty fucking Lesbo; she capped that guard— right?*" I.P.A. blurted.

"*Unlikely. I've met her. I can't see her ever leaving that condo of hers, the creepy fucking hermit. I'd bet she's agoraphobic,*" Moscow paused. "*Maybe some copycat running around out there, ya never know,*" Moscow said. "*Sorta like a live troll, I don't know.*"

"*This is so fucked,*" Boilermaker said. "*Now we've got murder tied to us. Why didn't they just shoot him in the fucking leg or something? Then we could have taken him. Fuck me.*"

"*Calm down, Boiler,*" Moscow said.

"*Nuh-uh, I say we cut ties with that crazy Lesbo bitch. Even if it wasn't her, she holds all the cards, man. She's got the addresses and dates of all the places we hit and the fucking murder weapon—possibly,*" Boilermaker said, catching the look from Moscow.

"*I said calm the fuck down, Boilermaker. We don't know for sure it was her, but I'll find out, believe me. I say we get our ten houses, then re-evaluate. I need at least that much more cash,*" Moscow paused. "*That's my vote in this fucking democracy anyway.*"

"*I don't know,*" I.P.A. said. "*I always stand with you Moscow, but Boilermaker's got a good point. Even if she didn't cap that fool, she's got way too much on us. She could be all up in our bank accounts for all we know. I ain't sayin' anything new, by the way.*"

Moscow began pacing. This brought a smile to Trusty's lips as did the hot rum.

"*I'm putting something together. When we break from Trusty*" *it's gotta be clean, otherwise she can put a real hurt on us."*

"What's the plan?" I.P.A. asked.

"Working on it."

"Bullshit," Boilermaker said, standing face to face with Moscow Mule. "Either that bitch is out or I am."

"Let me clarify. I've got us this far. I need that tenth house and I know you fucks do too."

As Boilermaker and Moscow Mule held the face-to-face, I.P.A. quietly asked, "Let's suppose it wasn't that weird Lesbo broad; who'd help us out like that? Who was in that fucking house with us—someone gunning for the kid? Or some kinda super fan of our gang? It kinda freaks me out."

"It won't matter after my plan kicks in, fools, believe me," Moscow barked, indicating the end of the conversation.

Trusty had been planning to move on from the tent gang but not before leaving a parting gift. She could be gone in sixty seconds, like that shitty Nicolas Cage movie—forty-five seconds actually. She paid cash month to month on the condo, a deal she solidified when she paid the first year's rent up front. Her possessions were few and the place came sparsely furnished. She had an equipment bag the size of a carry-on and a suitcase. Her place didn't look anything like the hacker pads in Hollywood movies. The place was museum-spotless. Her floors weren't covered in thick cables snaking all throughout her home like in films. Trusty could do everything from a single laptop and an external hard drive, and that was it.

Now that the crew was plotting her demise, she'd use the kid's death to her advantage.

Trusty was going to teach those ungrateful fucks what it was like to double-cross her. Then she'd be putting L.A. in her rearview.

CHAPTER FIVE

I didn't expect to learn anything from Cody's murder scene. I'd have been stuck behind the yellow tape with the reporters gaining little to no hard info and a bunch of theories and rumors. I decided to go back in time, specifically to the tent gang's seventh victim, the Kensington family. I logged onto Youtube and pulled up the footage of Mr. Shawn Kensington's interview on the local Channel 7 News. The Kensington address was pixelated but the street sign over the reporter's right shoulder was in view for a brief second. I paused the image on my computer and laser-focused on the street sign.

There you are, Belinda Court,. one thousand block, in Silverlake.

All that was left was pulling it up on Google Maps, hopping into the ol' gal and seeing what I could see.

Shawn Kensington was built like two fire hydrants glued together. His thick thighs bulged through his dark blue corduroys, and his dress shirt, a lighter shade of blue, clung to his short muscular torso. He carried his arms out further from his sides than necessary as if his Latissimus Dorsi muscles were pushing his arms out there. He easily could have gone up a half size in the original *Terminator* movie T-shirt to let the muscles breathe, but then the desired look would be off. He puffed out his chest, creased up his brow and worked his expression into a sneer.

"Can I help you?"

"I hope so, my name's Lou Crasher and—"

"Yeah, so?"

"I'm looking into the tent gang; in fact, I want to take 'em down. I understand they hit your place."

"I was robbed, yeah, but you don't look like a cop," he said, folding his arms across his chest and flexing the forearm muscles while purposely pushing out the biceps with his fists to make his arms look bigger. A wide stance, with toes pointed out slightly, said the real estate he stood upon—as well as confidence—were all his.

"I'm not a cop and I'll take it as a compliment that I don't resemble one. I'm looking into this for a client."

"So you're private."

"I'm a citizen who's lending a hand."

"Are ya any good?"

"Most would say so."

"Lemme see some I.D." He frowned briefly at my driver's license, then handed it back. "Well, ya might as well come on in cause I know the cops ain't gonna do shit. I've seen your address, so don't try any shit—payback's a bitch, Lou-Crasher-from-North-Hollywood." He snapped his neck to the side, cracking it for emphasis. I wondered if tough guys practice this stuff.

"Wouldn't dream of trying any shit," I said.

I stepped into a stylish open-concept home that was tastefully furnished. The setup was functional, no flashy shabby chic or excessive knickknacks. No clutter.

The first thing he wanted to show me was his oversized LG refrigerator. It was tagged in bright red spray paint, the tent gang's parting gift on all jobs.

The Tent Gang was here, sorry we missed you dumb bitches!

There was something there—a vibe of some sort—but I couldn't place it. It was much different seeing the desecration in person as opposed to on the television news.

"Why ya staring so hard, Crasher, ya got something? Ya see something?"

"Maybe. Would you mind showing me anything else that was vandalized, or show me where items were removed?"

"Sure, we'll start in my office. I work from home."

I followed him across the expanse of his great room.

"Nice floors, Shawn. Are they oak?"

"Nope," he said over his shoulder. "Engineered something or other the wife wanted. The shit ain't cheap, either."

"Well, beautiful just the same," I said.

"Ha! Beautiful in the magazine, beautiful in the showroom but a pain in both balls in real life."

"Oh?"

"Goddamn dust trap."

I gave them a closer look and noticed dusty footprints. "Shit," I said.

"Don't worry about your shoes, keep 'em on."

"No, I was going to ask, are these prints your kids'? They seem smaller than yours, what? Size nine?"

"Nine and a half," he clarified, chest puffed. "Wife and kids are up in Big Bear. They haven't been home since before the break-in."

He stopped dead in his tracks, got into a back-catcher's squat and looked down with a scowl.

"Did the cops take an interest in these?"

"If they did, they said shit to me about 'em, Mr. Crasher. I like where your head is at. The cop who was here couldn't blow outta here fast enough, and he damn well didn't show any concern over—"

He began removing his shoes, "here, let's take these off and backtrack to the kitchen, that's where they came in."

"How do you know that?"

"Roscoe's, the fumigators, called me the minute they noticed the tent was sliced. In fact, they didn't start dismantling it until I came screaming up here in my 'vette. I've seen the news stories; I knew how this match was going to end," he returned to the folded-arm stance.

We carried our shoes past the LG fridge. LG is a Korean-owned company. The LG stands for life's good—not so much for the Kensingtons.

"Obviously Roscoe's didn't want to be liable in any way for what might have happened in here," I said.

"Yeah, no shit, Crasher. Sorry, but no shit. These tent gang assholes have everybody freaked out."

We laid our shoes on a two-foot by three-foot mat dotted with several tiny sunflowers. We eased back, keeping to the edges of the floor, and surveyed the engineered material as if we were two guys looking for a contact lens. Shawn's slipper prints were easy to discern. I found a fresh imprint with a tread mark that appeared to feature a bold letter A: the cop's.

"Did the cop not go beyond the kitchen, Shawn? His prints seem to—"

"No, he mostly stood by the door and questioned me...the shit-prick," he mumbled.

"Why would you call him a—that?"

"The line of questioning was like I was trying to run an insurance scam or something."

"Really? That blows."

"Totally, I almost told him to F-off." He stood up straight with a far-off look in his eyes and filled his chest with air. "I should have told him to F-off, don't you think, Mr. Crasher?"

"I don't know, Shawn, I tend to think not much good comes from doing that to cops. You might have received a Maglite flashlight to the skull and your hands cuffed behind your back."

"Yeah, you're probably right," he sighed. "He can still F-off anyway."

I needed to move this interview off the 'F-off' trail. "So, what do you do that a guy can work from home?"

"I'm a stay-at-home dad—Mr. Mom all the way."

"Is that so?"

"No, I'm bullshitting you," he said. "It's just something I say to see how people react. Most guys judge, but you didn't. You might be all right, Mr. Crasher."

"I don't care if you're a stay-at-home dad. It's cool by me."

"It's just something I *say*. I'm not a—look I'm a writer."

"Nice. What do you write?"

"I write plot lines for professional wrestling."

"Now that sounds way cool," I said.

"Does it?" he spun toward me challengingly. "Act one: wrestler A knocks out referee. Wrestler B takes the opportunity to sneak up behind wrestler A and cold cock him with a folding chair. Referee regains consciousness. Disqualification. Match over. Real cool, Mr. Crasher. Real fucking cool," his voice ticked up at the end of the sentence.

"You look like you wrestled yourself back in the day," I said. The tiniest smile spread across his face for a moment. Nearly every upper body muscle contracted then released. It was the "little-big-man's" equivalent of a dog wagging its tail when it hears its name.

"Too friggin' short. And don't go suggesting midget wrestling, either," he said, pointing a finger at me, "I ain't that fuckin' short."

I held up my hands in surrender. My guess was that Shawn Kensington had dreams of being the Heavyweight Wrestling champ of the world until his size became an issue. Plan B probably involved writing the great American novel. When that didn't pan out, he moved over to, or perhaps down to, wrestling stories.

"You know, I'm getting your slipper prints but I'm not getting any worker boots or running shoes from the tenting crew—the fumigators, I mean."

"It's in their contract that any in-home work will be done with shoes off. I guess they kept their word, which is surprising, because blue-collar guys are usually shit-pricks."

Shawn Kensington was a picnic basket full of cynicism and rain clouds.

"Hang on," I said, taking a knee. "Are you seeing little smudge shapes in your area?"

Kensington adopted my pose, "Yes, yes I am. What the hell are we looking at?"

I stood back up and racked my brain. Shawn remained still, waiting for my answer. A picture was coming into focus.

"Ah, I know what this is. Last month a girl I dated dragged me to a bunch of open houses. Some of the realtors asked that we put these little disposable paper booties over our shoes. These are booty smudges, pal." I was proud of myself. I put my foot beside one of the bootie tracks.

"Okay, booties. What does this mean?"

"Are you sure the crew wore socks and not paper booties?"

"Yup, they even sent a short video. Weird, huh?"

"Then for one thing these bootie prints are about two and a half inches smaller than my foot, and I'm a size eleven."

"Okay, so that means they're short fucks like me."

"Agreed. Not that you're a short fuck but—" I let it hang on the air.

"Son of a bitch. What else? I mean, come on Crasher, you're the supposed P.I. here. We got little pricks in booties, what else? Let's go, I need answers."

Clearly, hanging around and writing for wrestlers had convinced Shawn that he'd gained some wrestler dimensions. I stared and said nothing.

"Sorry, I'm being an asshole. My wife says I can be such an asshole sometimes."

"She sounds like a keeper."

He over-laughed the way pro wrestlers do when they cut their promo videos.

"Okay, Shawn, let's see where your jazz was pinched, cool?"

"You got it, follow me."

Shawn took me to his office where he had a forty-eight-inch Vizio TV set on a pedestal; that is, until the "shit-pricks" stole it. A dusty imprint clearly marked where the TV had sat along with a few wires no longer wired up to anything. Back in the hall, we cut left and entered both boys' bedrooms, one after another. The thieves had lifted two tablets but left the chargers behind. I asked how Shawn knew the kids hadn't taken the devices with them. "Because they called and asked if I'd seen 'em—they forgot them, that's how," he said, irritated.

In the master bedroom Shawn showed me his huge walk-in closet. Two-thirds down the rack was a space where three Hugo Boss suits had formerly hung. Across the aisle, three pairs of women's stilettos no longer called the low-pile beige carpet home. Shawn Kensington could not remember the brand name. "Expensive as fuck" was all he could recall.

I got out my little black book and jotted down the Kensingtons' missing items, hoping this might illuminate a pattern. I also wrote up a quick note on the bootie aspect. Shawn walked with me on my way out, using his favorite "s-p" phrase three more times.

"Catch these guys, Crasher. I'd hire ya myself, but you've already got a client so—" he coughed, attempting to clear some phlegm. "My insurance is going to shake out all right, but just catch 'em, will ya? I hate all the free press they get."

"Here's my card, Shawn. Call me if you think of anything else."

He turned the card over in his chubby fingers.

"Says here you're a drummer."

"I am. Like I said, I'm not a licensed P.I., but rest assured I will nail these…what's your phrase again?"

"Shit-pricks," he said, with eyes lit up like runway landing lights.

I was about to make my way to the front door when I felt a little something, almost like a pebble, under my left foot. I moved it aside and saw a blue triangular-shaped piece of metal. I picked it up and was about to give it to Shawn to toss when I decided to ask him about it.

"Do you know what this belongs to?"

With eyes squinted he turned it over in his pudgy fingers.

"Beats my balls. Whadda you think?"

I took it back and examined it. "It's got a partially etched imprint here, recognize it?"

He pulled on a pair of reading glasses. "Looks like part of the letter U, or maybe double-U."

"Mind if I take it with me?"

"Go for it," he said.

I rolled away from the Kensington house at just under ten miles an hour. Out of my side mirror I could see Shawn on his phone, anxiously entering data. I made a right turn at the end of the street. My phone buzzed. I pulled over to read the text. It was from the man I'd just left.

Crasher, you need to buff out that stang man, then it'll be bitchin'. Maybe I'll show you my 'vette one day.

Shawn K.

CHAPTER SIX

It was nearing eight p.m., which meant I was way past my sandwich-and-beer hour. Los Angeles no longer has a set rush hour, or any hours for that matter, it just has traffic, plain, simple and relentless. The main routes are clogged, and the shortcuts suggested by apps are no longer short; they're just cuts. At least by eight it's more manageable than at mid-afternoon.

I had some pepper Toscana cheese that my good friend Kat had given me. She'd insisted that it was time for this amateur P.I. to move beyond sharp cheddar. Who was I to argue? I brought the cheese to the counter. I popped the tiny freezer open to discover that my loaf of twelve-grain had a decent-sized piece of bread and the heel.

"This brother needs to do some serious shopping," I mumbled.

In the back of the fridge I dug out a jar of roasted red peppers. Three little guys remained. I was still in luck. I had a teaspoon of mayonnaise and half as much hot mustard. Clearly, I was going to have to combine them. The egg carton surrendered three lone eggs. I brought those to the counter.

I put the bread into the toaster but didn't get the toast going just yet. I fried the eggs in a fifty-fifty split of olive oil and butter. I had to keep an eye on the eggs because those babies needed to come out over-easy. If those yokes hardened, then the nation might as well go to war—an added war. When the eggs took on the correct shade of white, I depressed the toaster lever. Timing is everything in life and in drumming as well.

The toast popped. I spread the mayo/mustard ration. I sliced the cheese thinly and laid them atop the slice of bread. The eggs were ready to rock. With my ancient spatula I eased them into position. Steam came off the yokes. Damn I was good. Another thin layer of cheese was piled on. I placed the three peppers crossways to the cheese, as sandwiches prefer a yin and yang style approach to particulate stacking.

Suddenly I realized I'd forgotten the fresh cracked black pepper. *Come on, Crasher, focus!* I removed the heel roof and blasted the black pepper into the sandwich and then refitted the roof with the deftness of a diamond setter.

Without further thought I headed to my couch, did a one-eighty, reached into the fridge and pulled out an ice-cold pilsner brewed by a local brewery in the beach cities. The first bite rocked my taste buds. When hot egg yolk drips onto a man's fingers he knows he's arrived. I took a healthy pull on the pilsner and nearly wept—what a pairing. I was all set for bite number two when my cell buzzed. I recognized the number.

"Mrs. Wiggins, how are you holding up? Shaken that cold yet?"

"I'm afraid not Louis, would you mind coming up and giving me a hand?"

"Of course not. I'll be up in—"

"I didn't catch you in the middle of a case or sandwich, did I?"

"Actually both, but they can wait."

"Nonsense, haul the sandwich with you and we'll eat together while we discuss your case. I could use the excitement."

"I'm not often called exciting, but I'll take it. See you in two."

In the beginning Violet Wiggins was the sweet old lady living above me who loaned me Rockford Files DVDs. As time went on, we became good friends and I discovered that she not only was my neighbor, but she owned the apartment building. Last week she came down with a cold and is having trouble shaking it.

Her door was ajar when I arrived.

"Mrs. Wiggins," I said with a knock. "It's Lou and one of his world-famous sandwiches."

"I'm back here," her voice scratchy with the cold.

I peeked into her kitchen as I passed by. The kettle was set to boil in minutes. I continued down the hall to her television room. She smiled weakly from her cloth recliner. A thick, checkered wool blanket covered her legs and partial torso.

"Don't get too close. I may still be contagious, Louis."

"Drummers and tough guys don't get colds, Mrs. Wiggins."

"Nonsense."

I offered her a bite of my sandwich, but she declined, saying she couldn't taste anything at the moment. When I broke down the ingredients for her, she put a slender hand out and shook it back and forth as if to say it sounded so-so as sandwiches go.

"Kettle's about to boil. Do you know which tea you'd like?" I asked.

"Yes, it's on the counter. Please add a little honey and lemon if you wouldn't mind."

"How 'bout a belt o' the sauce. It might kill the bad bugs in you."

"There's no booze in this house other than that beer you have there. Now stop fooling around and tell me about this case. It's been a while, hasn't it?"

"Couple of months, yes."

"Why are you smiling like that, Louis?"

"I'm doing this for Jake."

She sucked her air in and put a tiny hand to her chest.

"Well, why didn't you say so. Prop up this pillow, hand me my tea, then give me the skinny, will you?"

I got Violet comfortable then launched into the details of the case. She decided to join me in my meal and had me heat up the rest of the chicken soup she had on her stove. I was also instructed to bring her some crackers and the butter dish.

I called from the kitchen, "Oh look, I found a bottle of sherry under the sink," I teased. "Are you sure you don't want a little medicinal—"

"You shouldn't lie to an old lady, Louis, now hurry back and finish off your story."

I managed to get all the details out, pausing only to finish my sandwich and chase it with the pilsner. Violet insisted on buttering her own crackers. As I watched her thin hand grip the small knife, I admired how she meticulously spread the butter over every inch of the cracker without a hint of a tremble in her hand. It gave me comfort. Although in her mid-eighties, Mrs. Wiggins was going to be here for a good while. She dipped half the cracker into the bowl then looked at me as she took a bite.

"What? Why are you staring at me like that, Louis?"

"Nothing. I'm just—"

"It's just a cold, Louis. I'm fine—not going anywhere."

She slurped more soup and repeated the cracker routine two more times. We sat in silence. I was finished with my sandwich.

"Right," she said, once she was done. "As I'm sure you can imagine, I have a few thoughts."

"Great."

"But first, if you go into my fridge you'll find a big jug of orange juice."

I got up, "I'll get you a glass."

"No, thank you, but behind the container is a little something for you."

When I came back from the kitchen, she had a giant smile on her face.

"This is the pilsner I drink. You do have booze in the house."

"Beer isn't booze," she said.

"I often say the exact same—"

"It's why I said it. Do you mind clearing these plates?"

"Happy to."

When I returned the blanket on her legs was tucked tighter

and her hands were folded in her lap.

"Now then, have a seat, put a coaster under that beer bottle and listen with both ears."

CHAPTER SEVEN

On Monday, August sixteenth, Jake reported to the L.A. Superior Court-Van Nuys East at eight a.m. He was an hour early. Judge Dana Bhatri was a fifty-five-year-old, no-nonsense judge of Nepali descent. By eleven a.m. she'd heard four cases and cleared them with her reputed expediency. Jake knew of her rough-and-tumble style. She was tough but it bothered Jake little because she was fair, no one denied that.

"Jake Strickland, you have waived your right to counsel, is that correct?"

"Correct, your honor."

With a heavy sigh she slowly shifted her eyes to the prosecuting attorney. "And Ms. Gilbert, does your client still wish to press charges?"

"Yes, your honor, my client was brutally assaulted by—"

Judge Bhatri held up her left hand, traffic-cop style, while jotting down a note.

"Ms. Gilbert, we're not at closing arguments and there is no jury here this day." It was a stern warning. Jake had read that Janie Gilbert was known as a grandstander.

"Excuse me, judge! Excuse me!" A woman's voice came from the back of the courtroom. The bailiff who'd apparently been daydreaming was too slow to get to the woman. Jake turned his muscled frame toward the woman who raced down the aisle, and he recognized her. Judge Bhatri looked annoyed.

"Excuse me, your honor, sorry to barge in, but I was on that plane and I want to stand up for him, for Jake, I mean. Or I'd like to vouch for him—a sort of character witness—that's it, I want to be a character witness," she said, puffing and adjusting her power suit.

The bailiff was almost to the interloper. "It's all right Clarence, no sense earning your keep now. Let her approach. And promise me that one day you'll teach me how to sleep with *my* eyes open the way you do. It might make my days go faster."

Laughter rolled through the courtroom. Clarence blushed. The judge brought her gavel down rapidly twice.

Jake let his mind drift back to the event that had landed him in Judge Bhatri's courtroom.

Jake sat on the 727 plane two rows up from the rear washroom. He was on his way back home from Phoenix. The stepson of a long-time acquaintance had gotten himself in a jam. The acquaintance had called Jake and pleaded for help, and Jake had agreed to help—one last time. The acquaintance would no doubt call again in six or seven months; the boy was a screwup. When the next call came Jake would not be on the other end of the line, he was done.

Jake had the window seat, which he preferred. One might assume that someone like Jake would be more partial to the aisle seat for the ease of escape but Jake was agile, so where he sat mattered little. Having brought his own nourishment of mixed nuts, carrots and water, Jake politely declined the rail-thin flight attendant's offering off her cart. Jake's seatmate, a Greek businessman with a size thirty-eight waist, small torso and thinning hair ordered a vodka-cranberry—his second. After completing the first highball, the businessman had folded up the spreadsheet he had been studying and tucked it into his tiny purse-style carry-on. The way the man glanced over at Jake and smiled from time to time told Jake that the gent was mere moments away from attempting conversation. Jake took the opportunity to feign sleep. Within two minutes the man, apparently overcome with boredom, reached back into his purse and brought out his smart phone. Jake grinned inwardly; grownups of today were fast becoming toddlers in the attention-span department.

A commotion rumbled from somewhere near the front of the plane. Jake kept his eyes closed but focused his hearing. He blocked out the engine noise, the conversation being held by two female coeds across the aisle, and the food cart brake being set. What he did hear was the voice of a male who was upset at another male for sneezing on him. Alcohol in both their voices lobbed several threats. The flight attendant left the cart and tried her best to ebb the tide. One of the men called her a bitch.

Another male voice farther back, which meant he was closer to Jake's row, told the squabblers to "sit the fuck down." He was African American. A woman screamed, which meant the incident had escalated to a dangerous point—the squabblers were now tussling. Two guys having such a beef on the street or in a bar would be no big deal, but on a plane with nervous passengers in a post-911 world—potential disaster. Jake opened his eyes.

"Excuse me, sir," Jake said to his seatmate, "would you mind handing me your beverage, standing up, and moving to your left into the aisle?"

"What? What are you going to do? There's a fight or—"

"Never mind, stay put," Jake said, and with that he grabbed the man's cocktail and folded up his tray in one fluid motion. Ducking his head, he stepped over the seated man, first one foot then the other. The man held up his hands as if ordered by a police officer. Once in the aisle, Jake spun and handed the man his cocktail.

"Remember, stay put," Jake ordered softly yet sternly.

The businessman nodded as he watched Jake move down the aisle. He then leaned over to the two coeds.

"Girls, check this out, I believe it is going to be awesome."

The coeds stood up with their phones and began shooting. Jake moved smoothly but with purpose, the slight turbulence having no visible effect. He moved like a naval captain, unfazed by choppy seas.

Jake got three seats from the fight when a large man in full denim with a big gut hanging over his Florida-shaped belt buckle fell in behind him and tapped him firmly on his shoulder. Jake was annoyed by the interruption, especially because the two combatants up front were beginning to throw big punches. When Jake turned, Florida Belt Buckle's lady friend shrieked at seeing the look on his face. Florida Belt Buckle flinched but stood his ground.

"I'm comin' with ya, partner, and you can't stop me."

"Can't I?"

The man shot out a palm in an attempt to shove Jake's chest. Jake knew the Floridian was trying to show his lady what he was made of, but his tough-guy shove never made it to target. Jake's left hand shot forward and grabbed the man low by his floating rib. Powerful fingers dug in and gave a hefty tug. Such a maneuver delivers the sensation that the rib is about to be ripped from the cage. The man yelped. Tears immediately ran down both cheeks. His female partner went full-blown hysterical.

"Quiet!" Jake shouted and pointed at her with his free hand. With a sharp inward breath and tears rushing to her eyes, the woman fell silent.

Once Jake had the big man back in his seat, he apologized to them both but assured them things would get worse if the man followed Jake into the fight. The big man panted heavily while nodding several times—message received. Then he said something through clenched teeth that Jake could have cracked all of his ribs for: "What if they're terrorists? The black one might be Muslim." Five nearby passengers called out with varying forms of gasps at the mention of the T-word. This was exactly what Jake had feared.

"Everybody stay calm this will be over in a moment," he said, hoping that would suffice.

The two scrappers had managed to make it into the aisle for more fighting space. Panic was building throughout the plane. A flight attendant was knocked back toward the cockpit. She staggered and would have gone to the floor if a fit woman in her early thirties hadn't broken her fall. The battlers were larger than

Jake had initially thought. Both were in their late twenties, one black, the other caucasian, both around six-two, two-twenty.

Jake didn't waste any time. He approached the black fighter whose back was to him, reached up and pulled him around by the chin and head. It's always easy to maneuver a man by the skull; if it hadn't been for the fight, it would have looked as though the two were politely trading places. Jake was now between the fighters. The man Jake had moved was shocked but recovered quickly and came at him. Jake scarcely glanced back at him as he fired off a backward kick, catching the man squarely in the stomach. He heard him drop with a cough. With hands casually at his sides Jake took a measured step toward the caucasian, who charged him with a yell. Jake met him head-on by leaping forward. As combatants collided, Jake slammed the man's head into the overhead carrier bin. The man was dazed and stumbled back, but Jake didn't give him a chance to recover. He leaped forward again with a superman punch and caught the man on the button. He was out before he slumped against the bulkhead.

Without hesitation the fit woman who had earlier helped the flight attendant asked for a spare pair of seat belts and began binding the big man's wrists. Jake winked at her. Just then somebody yelled, "Behind you!"

The first combatant was coming in hot. Jake turned and stood in a fighting stance. The man slowed down, realizing the element of surprise was lost, and that to charge the skilled brother when he was ready for it wasn't wise. The man threw two lame jabs that obviously weren't meant to be serious. In fact, Jake lowered his hands and avoided the jabs with the tiniest of head weaves.

The man then fired off a straight right aimed at Jake's face. Jake slipped it, came in close and gave him a powerful hammer strike to the collarbone. He winced but answered with his opposite elbow. It nearly caught Jake on the ear. They separated. The big man threw a high kick that Jake blocked with his shoulder and biceps. Jake was impressed by the fact that the man had the agility to launch the kick in such a tight space.

However, he'd still make him pay for it. Another two phony jabs and the man attempted the same high kick. This time Jake caught the leg; wrapped his left arm around the attacker's foot and ankle, and with lightning speed, delivered two fast, hard shots to the man's right knee. The man screamed. Then Jake kicked the man in his other knee and let him drop to the floor. The man writhed and screamed in the aisle. Onlookers cheered from behind a dozen cell phones. Wonderful, Jake thought, attention. He turned, looking for the woman who had tied up the first fighter.

"Looking for me?" she said from behind. She was holding another pair of spare seatbelts.

Jake picked up the man and walk-carried him to the exit row mid-plane and told the occupants they needed to move. They didn't argue. Jake lowered him into a seat, belted him in and tied his wrists to the arms rests. Next Jake put the other fighter up front across from Fit Lady and headed back to his own seat. He ignored the "thank yous" and attempted high fives. The flight attendant who had been knocked down earlier showed up and thanked him. She said the captain was speaking with the two men now and would be back later to speak to him. A minute later Fit Lady reappeared and stood over the businessman sitting beside Jake.

"Sir," she said, "I'm going to have to ask you to trade seats with me."

The businessman looked pleadingly at Jake. He got a flat expression in return. With a heavy sigh he grabbed his carry-on and man purse, and moved down the aisle. The fit woman sat down beside Jake.

"Alone at last," she said, beaming at Jake.

"Suits me," Jake said.

CHAPTER EIGHT

The clouds dotted the sky as if a painter had touched up his artwork as he headed out the door in a hurry. Occasionally a puffy cloud would float in front of the sun but had little effect on cooling the eighty-nine-degree heat. The GPS had me drive over the hill and descend into Hollywood. With windows down the warm breeze was doable, averaging seventy miles an hour, but once on the Hollywood streets the Mustang's interior was toaster-oven hot. Someday I'd have to install AC...someday.

My destination was The Knife Shoppe. I was betting that the little piece of ceramic shard I'd found at the Kensington house was from a knife blade. Mrs. Wiggins backed me on the play as well.

The store's AC was a welcome slap to the jawbone.

"What can I do for ya?" At six-three the counterman couldn't have weighed more than one-forty—even after eating a sixteen-ounce T-bone. His rolled-up sleeves revealed sinewy forearms that seemed to be swallowed up by cord-like veins. He put his hands down on the counter and leaned forward. I noticed the fourth finger of his right hand was missing from the middle knuckle down.

I placed the piece of metal on the glass countertop. The counterman connected two sides of his magnetic reading glasses together and examined the shard.

"It's from a Gintai knife. How did it break?"

"Gin—"

"Gintai is the brand."

"Sounds Asian, like the Ginsu," I said.

"And like the Ginsu, this ain't Asian either. It's just marketing. Ginsu was manufactured in Fremont, Ohio, and this little baby," he said, holding it up, "is made right here up in the Simi Valley."

"Well what do ya know about that?"

"A thing or two."

I considered hauling out my book but thought I'd trust my memory for now.

"How do the Gintais rate?"

"I'm gonna say middle-of-the-road on this one."

"Got any here?"

"Hang on," he said, and moved to a smart tablet. As his fingers tickled the screen, I checked out the joint. There were knives in the glass case as well as in cases behind him, not unlike a gun shop. I didn't see any colored ceramic knives in the store. He spun the tablet around for me to see.

"Here's your guy."

He'd pulled up the website and allowed me to scroll around briefly. The knife came in two sizes with a promise of more products to come. The color options were blue, red and orange with the colors flowing from handle to tip, one solid color. None of the knives were your standard stainless steel.

"This is great. Thanks for showing me this."

"Not at all. What's your interest?"

I didn't answer. "Say, these handles seem on the smaller size."

"Some people like a smaller grip," he said, reaching for the tablet. My time was up. "You never said what your interest in the knife was."

"Shopping for my ex-girlfriend," I lied. "Trying to win her back," I said, heading for the door.

"Hey, I can get the Gintai, have it here in two days. If not, I've got plenty other brands." He was off suspicious mode and back into salesman mode.

"I gotta think it over. She was eyeing a handbag by some Coach company or other. I may go with that."

I had my hand on the doorknob.

"Go with both," he said to my back. "Buy the bag and stick a paring knife in there as a surprise."

"Not a bad idea."

Other than it's a horrible idea. She reaches into the bag and slices her hand all to hell while checking out the compartments. Come on, dude.

"I'll let you know."

CHAPTER NINE

Meredith Billups was "friends" with her son on Facebook and they followed each other on Instagram. It was the only way the strict mother would allow his participation on the social media sites. This fact allowed me to search through Cody's social footprint. It felt weirdly intrusive tiptoeing through a dead man's online backyard, but if I found something that got me closer to the killer or killers then so be it. Cody had lots of friends and followers. His smile was infectious. His football buds were easy to pick out, but he also had many female friends. At first pass none appeared to be a serious girlfriend. But after twenty minutes of sifting through his life and doubling back in spots, there seemed to be one woman that popped up with some regularity. My guess was they were serious, because they were often alone with the shots either being selfies or pictures in restaurants and pubs where it seemed obvious that a server, hostess or bartender had played photographer. With Cody's other women friends, he was usually in groups doing the hangout thing.

Cody and the solo date seemed to care about each other, no question, but in some pictures there was an almost sadness, or at least seriousness, to their expressions. Something had occurred or was to occur.

Who are you, sweetheart?

I expanded my search to include the many friends tagged in his pictures and that produced a big hit. A recent photo of a handful of people gathered around a memorial to Cody. I recognized two of the guys, more from the clothes and body language than faces, as two guys close to Cody. I zoomed in on the background and saw a sign that read: *Go Beach*. I opened a second window and fed the phrase into Google.

Aha, Cal State Long Beach.

The shrine was on the Long Beach campus. I checked the time, then grabbed my keys. It was time to go to school.

I didn't bother with campus parking, fearing I'd have to sell a snare drum to cover the cost since as I didn't have a student parking pass. The decision had me crawling side streets for close to two months before I found a spot. After a ten-minute walk I was on campus with a prop backpack slung over my left shoulder. I certainly wasn't freshman age but convinced myself that I looked the perfect part of adult student circling back to grad school after a short stint in the workforce. I walked semi-aimlessly for the length of two football fields before I found the memorial. The area seemed larger than the photo I'd seen. A woman no more than twenty-one rested on bended knee and sniffled as she dropped a rose in between two candles.

"Just doesn't seem right," I said as I stepped up to her. She stood abruptly, clearly startled.

"Huh? I can't, I just can't," she said, and hurried off in the opposite direction. It gave me enough time to realize she wasn't Cody's close friend or any of the friends I'd seen in the various pictures. I took a knee, then pulled a handful of flowers from my pack and placed them between a photo of Cody with a group of friends laughing in a selfie and a tall glass candleholder. Keeping my phone low, I did a quick photo sweep of the entire shrine. Not wanting to overstay my welcome I stood and moved to a bench twenty yards away. Keeping up with the props, I hauled a political science book out of my backpack and adopted a studious student pose in case the campus cops came around. Tucked inside the book was an issue of L.A. Stix, a local drum magazine. The plan was to pass the time until one of Cody's buds I recognized stopped by. I scanned random articles until I came across a small piece done on Yesterday's Pop Tart. The author of the article described me as a hard hitter with a smooth groove. What more could I ask? She went on to say that although my backing vocals were not nearly as strong as my playing, they were getting better with each show. It was higher praise than I deserved.

As I began an article about the drummer from Blood Bath, a metal band with female drummer Little Katrina Kraft, of whom I'm a big fan, two young black guys in low sagging jeans, beige Timberland boots and oversized jackets approached the shrine. Both wore their afros blown way out and each had a single wireless white ear bud in his right ear. I'd seen them in a handful of pictures with Cody, only now the trio was down to a duo. I stowed my book and strolled over.

"Shit sucks, huh fellas?"

"Fuck yeah it does," the taller of the two said without taking his eyes off the memorial.

"I sure hope dey catch the punk-ass bitches that did dis," his partner said.

"Yup," I agreed.

The short one turned to me. "How you know Cody?"

"I didn't."

"The fuck you doin' here den, nigga?" Both buddies put eyes on me.

"Easy guys, I'm looking into this."

"You a reporter or some shit?"

"Nah, private. I wanna nail the cats that did this. I saw you guys on social, obviously you guys were tight with Cody."

"Hell yeah, we was," the taller one said, inching closer to me. I was slightly surrounded.

"You guys look linebacker-size. Y'all play together?" I asked.

"Compton Bears comin' up, LBC Dawgs after that." They fist-bumped.

"Cody was a running back," I said. "I hear he was badass."

"Nigga was a stud," the shorter one said. His eyes bulged slightly, like a Boston Terrier's. We turned back to the shrine.

"You lookin' into this for his moms?"

"Yeah, for Meredith," I said, wanting them to know I knew Cody's mother. After a minute of silence, the tall one asked me how they could help.

"You think this was random—wrong place, wrong time—or was someone gunning for him? Any enemies y'all know of?"

They said everybody liked Cody. No enemies. He was also a good student.

"And he was doin' good, too, until—"

"Shut the fuck up, Chicken," the taller one barked.

"A good student until, the incident?" I asked.

"Nah, not that, dude. He was doin' aight until he got popped."

The tall one gave Chicken a swift punch to the shoulder. "Squash that shit bruh, we don't know dis dude."

"I told you I'm working for Meredith. I'm on your side for fuck sakes," I said. "Popped for what?"

"Addie."

"You mean Adderall?" I asked remembering a documentary I'd seen where kids on campuses across the country used the "upper" to help them study...and party.

"That's the one. Cody be slingin' on campus and got ratted out by some fool. Campus 5-O shut it down and Cody got suspended."

"Dat's the reason he be workin' that security job. Ain't no way his moms would let him sit around until he come back here," the tall one added.

"Whole thing was bullshit, yo. White kids be sellin' all over this bitch but it's the nigga gets popped."

"I heard that," I said, bonding.

The taller one shot me a screwy look. "Nigga, where you from? You talk all funny n shit?"

"Canada." No sense lying.

"Shit, you a long way from home."

"Bout fifteen hundred miles," I said. "Anything else you guys can add?"

They had nothing other than a warning that if I was working for Meredith Billups, I'd better come correct because she doesn't play. I handed each of them my business card.

"Drummer? I thought you was a private eye, yo?"

"Gotta wear multiple hats in this economy bruh," I said.

"Whatever," the tall one said, before they moved on their way.

CHAPTER TEN

Judge Dana Bhatri held up a hand to quiet all in the courtroom. She removed her half-lens glasses and rubber her eyes. Prosecutor Janie Gilbert became frustrated and attempted to speak but was silenced. The more she irritated the judge the better for him, Jake thought. With a deep sigh the judge addressed the courtroom.

"Ladies and gentlemen my automatic coffee maker, which is set to brew at six a.m. didn't work this morning, not so much as a drop. It was then that I knew this was going to be one of those days. Mr. Strickland has chosen to represent himself, a situation that, although highly inadvisable for the accused, is perfectly legal and is his right. Being that Mr. Strickland, up to this point, is not calling any witnesses, I'm going to do something that might possibly send Ms. Gilbert here into a whirlwind. That being said, the court recognizes her objection in advance. The character witness will now step into the box and be sworn in."

Janie Gilbert leapt to her feet. "Your honor, I most certainly do object. We had no prior notification—"

"Can it, Gilbert, I've already acknowledged your objection. Were you not listening? Or were you asleep like my bailiff Clarence over there?"

The lawyer sat down in a huff and ruffled some papers. Clarence shifted from foot to foot and put his head down. The judge motioned for the witness to move to the witness box. The court clerk swore her in.

"Very good. Now then, Ms. Cox, please give the court your account of what happened on the airplane that day. Ms. Gilbert, I will allow a moderate amount of objections and interruptions but keep it to a minimum—I caution you."

As Heather Cox moved through the story Jake appreciated the way the judge made the witness feel at ease. Janie Gilbert was unable to keep her objections at a minimum and paid for it with several reprimands.

Heather completed her account and was thanked by the judge. Janie Gilbert rose and was about to put her questions to the witness but threw a curve ball at the judge and Jake as well.

"Your honor, before I question this witness, the People have an issue with the accused's stated occupation."

"Says here Mr. Strickland is a consultant. What is the issue Ms. Gilbert?"

"Your honor, my office has searched far and wide on this man and we can't find a single shred of evidence, if you will, as to what he consults in. In fact, we cannot find anything on him. It's as though he does not exist."

The judge asked Jake to rise.

"Okay, Mr. Strickland, what of it? What exactly is your occupation?" the judge asked.

"Your honor, I'd like to see you and counsel in your chambers if I may," Jake said.

"You're going to have to give the court more than that to get me out of this chair, Mr. Strickland."

"It's about my occupation. It's sensitive and may not be for the record."

"I knew it. I knew it was going to be one of those days. Ms. Gilbert, Clarence, Mr. Strickland and the stenographer will follow me to my chambers. I have a feeling where this is going," the judge said.

The people in the courtroom waited exactly nine minutes

before the door that led to the judge's chambers swung open. They witnessed a pissed-off prosecutor storm back into the courtroom. Jake took his seat. The plaintiff looked confused and asked his lawyer what was happening. Janie Gilbert wouldn't answer him. Clarence asked all in attendance to rise. Finally, the judge entered and sat down. With a stern voice she asked counsel, Jake and the plaintiff to "please stand."

"Ladies and gentlemen, just about anything can happen in a court of law and today, well, the unusual has occurred. Air travel can be a real bear as I'm sure most of you know. In particular it can be unsettling when an in-flight disturbance such as the one we heard about today occurs. Planes can be rerouted or worse," the judge said, pausing.

"The people on flight A35 owe a debt of gratitude to Mr. Strickland for the manner in which he diffused a potentially dangerous situation."

Janie Gilbert sighed loudly and was cautioned for it.

"Due to the sensitive nature of Mr. Strickland's occupation and his relationship with the United States government I am hereby dismissing the case against Jake Strickland. On behalf of the court and me personally, I'd like to thank Mr. Strickland for his service and the work he does. It's been a pleasure having you in my courtroom, Mr. Strickland. You are free to go."

CHAPTER ELEVEN

Rehearsal rooms in Los Angeles are rarely completely sound-proof but decent spots will at least deaden the sounds of the average rock band. As I approached room A of Awesome Sound Studios, I heard voices but not the singing kind. The band was called Yesterday's Pop Tart. I started out as a gun for hire, gigging a couple times per month with the group until the regular drummer's coke habit led to crystal methamphetamine and finally rehab. The band voted unanimously to give me the permanent spot on the drum throne. That was three months ago.

The words coming from room A were heated. I opened the door and stepped inside. Our fearless bandleader Tracy Sanderson stood six inches from Chalk, the bass player, and was laying into him with finger pointing at his chest. Fillmore, the guitar player, noodled quietly up and down the fret board of his guitar with head shaking right and left. I moved to the provided drum set and began putting my cymbals on stands.

"So you're not only quitting, you're going back to that asshole? Are you insane?" Tracy demanded.

"He's changed, Tracy, people do change, you know."

"Not that guy."

"He deserves a second chance," Chalk said with little conviction.

"Like fuck he does," Tracy said, and stormed over to her microphone stand.

"What's up?" I finally asked, breaking the silence.

"Loverboy here is going back to his boyfriend in Michigan," Tracy said.

"Wasn't he the cat that got your dog, um…there was an accident?" I asked, vaguely remembering a story Tracy had told me.

"Yes, *that* asshole," Tracy said. Fillmore nodded in agreement.

"Shut up all of you," Chalk shouted. "Fuck!"

Fillmore weighed in, "Yes, Lou, Carl took Chalk's Shih Tzu Rhino into the large dog pen area at a dog park where he was attacked by a Doberman. The little guy didn't survive it—unfortunately."

"Dang." I said.

"And he apologized a thousand fucking times—now can we rehearse for my last show, please? Jee-zus! Carl and I are going to try again and that's final, not that it's anyone's fucking business."

Tracy spoke low, "He didn't give a shit about the dog and he didn't give a shit about you either when he cheated on you, but if that's who you want—"

Chalk faced Tracy with arms stiff at his sides. "I don't give a shit about you or this band, okay? But I'm willing to play out tomorrow's show, so can we get to fucking work or fucking not?" His voice was in the Adele soprano range on the last word.

Tracy looked like she was going to pop him right in the nose. Their faces were almost close enough for a kiss. Tracy's body shook slightly with rage.

"Lou, count us in on ACDC's Back in Black, please. Mother fu—"

"One, two, three Hyaah!"

CHAPTER TWELVE

The next day at the Practice Joint flew by as days tend to do when I have a gig the same evening. One customer, a band called Cuckoos Nest, was short by a couple of dollars. They were longtime regulars so I let it slide with a friendly reminder of the policy. As they departed, I overheard the keyboard player mention that I was bringing attitude ever since becoming manager. If not for the fact that the Joint was a ground-level building, I'd have thrown him down a flight of stairs and shown him what attitude was.

As I was getting ready to leave, I heard a gurgling sound coming from the women's washroom. I knocked first, even though I knew it was empty. The first toilet was overflowing like Niagara Falls, thanks to a feminine napkin. Susie showed up at that moment.

"Hey, glad you're here, can you grab the plunger and mop and handle this?"

"Well I could," she giggled. I looked closely at her and noticed her pupils were doing creative gymnastics.

"Jesus, you're dusted. I'll do it," I said. "Go let Rat Bastard into room E."

As I shoved past her, she offered a giggled apology, then moved zombie-like down the hall. Some of the other co-workers called her Sloshie Susie, Susie Sauced or just plain Sloshie on account of she's always plastered on something.

The bathroom took me twenty minutes to handle. This put me behind schedule for my gig with the Tarts.

"Hey, hey it's late, Lou," Gino the soundman said as I climbed the steps to the stage. We fist-bumped.

"S'up, Gino?"

"You're normally first guy on stage. I hope it's not a bad omen."

"You really want to say that to a guy minutes before his show?" I said.

"Sorry, I'm being a dumb shit," he said. I didn't disagree. I adjusted the height of my snare drum while he affixed a microphone to it. As he clipped more mics to drums, I placed my cymbals where I liked them to be.

"Dang, Lou, that was quick," Gino said.

"It's a little thing I like to call professionalism," I said with a wink.

"Guess I'll go get the rest of the—"

"We're right here," Tracy said, stepping onto the stage from the green-room area. She and Gino embraced. With the lads plugged in and tuned up Tracy called us together just in front of my kit.

"All that shit from last night doesn't matter—never happened. It's all about right now, just like every gig. Let's kick the shit out of this crowd," she said, and put her hand into the center of the group. We thrust hands on top of hers and called, "Fucking Tarts" as a chorus. It was corny but surprisingly, it got us fired up at every show. Tracy gave Gino the thumbs up. As I headed back to my kit Tracy spanked my ass and blew me a kiss when I spun around. This was new. Hmm.

Gino gave us a grand intro over the P.A. system, then hit the necessary switch to raise the curtain. The place was packed. When the crowd saw Tracy decked out in chunky black boots, fishnet stockings, the mini-est of black leather miniskirts and a crop top that made me glad to be a man, they cheered like she was Beyonce. Tracy's body was somewhere between gymnast and figure-skater firm. She was built for observation and hands-on inspection.

I was already into my phat mid-tempo groove by the time the curtain was up to the rafters. Tracy stepped to the mic and let her hips sway side to side. With arms stretched out to the sides she snapped her fingers to my beat. As I dug deeper into the groove, she put more music into her hips. I wasn't sure if I was driving her movement or she was driving my groove. Either way, the crowd noise rose another ten decibels.

"Club Zoot how're ya doooooooin'?" she called. The audience roared in response.

"To be honest, I almost forgot to say hi to you poor bastards. That phat groove my drummer's laying down does something to me. That pounding rhythm you feel in your chest...and my girlie parts, is brought to you by the one and only Lou Crasher, give him love, bitches!"

The crowd showed their appreciation, which was the cue for Chalk to join me with his funky bass line. He stepped to the front of the stage, got low and slapped his bass like it was his teenaged son who'd crashed his new car. Between the two of us we got the head bopping to turn into full-on dancing. Tracy introduced Chalk, which in turn brought guitar player, Filmore, into the song. Tracy introduced him as Jimi Hendrix's red headed stepson...even though his hair was dyed turquoise blue. We jammed awhile until I swung my microphone in front of my face.

"Ladies, gentlemen and genders that rock where ya rock, I introduce not only the hottest member of this band but possibly the sexiest damn piece o' certified come-get-some up in this bar. Oh, and by the way, she sings like a mutha. Maybe ya'll didn't hear me," I paused. "I said she sings like a MUTHA!"

That amped the crowd up. "I give you Tracy 'tonight's the night' Sanderson!"

Tracy grabbed her mic and improvised with some wailing and old school scat. She owned the room, belting on for close to two minutes before giving me the subtle signal: the rock 'n' roll hand sign low at her thigh. I hurled into a giant drum fill over the toms, incorporating the bass drum along the way until I stopped on beat one like a freight train colliding with the side of a mountain. From there we segued into a funk rock version of Jill Scott's *Golden*. When we were done, Chalk leaned over to me and shouted, "This crowd is going ape-shit, bro! Fucking ape-shit!"

The next two songs were originals written by Tracy. The audience lapped them up like a group of thirsty Labrador Retrievers. During song four, which was our funky version of ACDC's Back in Black, a sexy Latina with mean eyes alternated between giving me, then Tracy, lusty looks. I gave her my pearly whites with bedroom eyes. Tracy caught it and wagged a "naughty boy" finger at me.

"Zoot Suiters! Thanks for coming out on a fucking Tuesday night by the way," she said, adjusting the mic stand.

"This next song is one I wrote called Cat Face. See, I used to have this orange tabby that liked to sleep with me. She'd snuggle at my feet but in the morning, she'd always be on my head. So I'd wake up almost suffocated with cat hair all in my hair and on my face. So one morning a guy I was seeing came over early, right? So I open the door and he says, 'good morning, Cat Face'. What a dick—right?"

The crowd agreed.

"So, there we are in the middle of boning and I grab him by the nads and tell him if he ever calls me Cat Face again it's no more cookie for him. And believe me, Zoot Suiters," she paused with a smile, "this cookie is delicious!" she said, pointing to the front of her mini skirt with both hands shaped to look like guns.

"Fucking Cat Face, count us in, Lou!" she shouted. And so I did.

Six songs later my buddy Bobby Coldwater staggered to the stage and shouted, "You're smoking hot!"

"Thank you, kind, drunk sir," Tracy said.

Without hesitation I took a spare drumstick and launched it end over end at Bob. It hit him square in the chest. He seemed confused until our eyes met. I gave him a warning look. I'd totally forgotten I'd invited him to the show. He smiled and repeated his line to Tracy, then turned to me and shouted, "Fuck you Lou, you suck!"

Coming in hot from his left was the Motorhome-sized bouncer known as Moose. He put a meaty hand to Bob's neck, which looked like a chicken bone in Moose's big paw, and guided him through the crowd. The audience applauded the move.

"Don't hurt him, Moose, that's my future deadbeat baby daddy right there," Tracy said getting a big laugh from her fans.

Three songs later we were finished and packed up and in the parking lot. Tracy was about to pay us when the hot Latina from earlier approached.

"Great show," she said.

We thanked her.

"I was wondering if you two would like to come back to my place for a drink?"

"Tempting," Tracy said. "But we're beat, maybe another time."

The thirty-something beauty with the mean eyes kissed each of us on our cheeks. I took an involuntary step forward...I think. The Latina beauty queen then hopped into a Mustang Boss 302. It rumbled to life. She tossed a wave then rolled out of the lot.

"Shame, I love that car."

"Pervert," Tracy said and punched me on the shoulder.

She paid us out, then we gave awkward hugs to Chalk and wished him all the best with his Michigan man. It was down to Tracy and me.

"I guess that's it then."

"Uh-huh. You coming?" she asked.

"Excuse me?"

"You're kinda slow on the uptake, aren't you Crasher."

"At times."

She stepped close to me. "I sent hot little J-Lo away because I don't want to share you with her."

"I—"

Her lips collided with mine. The kiss was hot, wet and a little boozy. We pulled apart briefly then went at it again, only harder.

"You did refer to me as 'tonight's the night' so, my place, follow me," she said breathlessly.

I tried to play it cool but only managed, "yes, follow, place, yes."

CHAPTER THIRTEEN

Tracy barely reached five -two in heels but she was a mini mouse of energy and passion. I'm not a guy who uses the word insatiable often but that was Tracy; she truly couldn't get enough. She was great for my ego with her repeated "yeses," "don't stops" and "fuck me Crashers." Anytime I settled into a rhythm, she'd pull an acrobatic move, putting us into a new position, giving the whole sex symphony a Cirque du Soleil vibe. She liked being in control, and to be honest, I dug where she led. And I'd be lying if I said I didn't learn a thing or two. Always learning—isn't that what the Buddhists say?

"I knew you'd rock," she said as we panted on our backs.

"I suspected the same of you."

"Suspected? Oh, slow down with the hot talk, Crasher, you're getting me all wet again."

"Correction, I knew you'd be a little firecracker, a hell cat, a delicious dervish in the sack but—"

"But what?"

"Jumping band members usually ends messy. At least for me in the past, so I wasn't trying to make any moves—probably why I didn't see you coming."

She slowly climbed on top of me.

"Here's how it won't get messy," she said, slowly moving her hips back and forth and in slow circles.

"No strings. I call; you come over and knock the bottom out of me. If you call;" she paused and increased the tempo of her hip moves, "well, we'll just have to see if I'm available or not."

"Doesn't sound like equality to me," I said.

She smiled and turned up the heat. "You want equality, fuck a dyke peacenik."

"I don't think they'd dig the Crasher," I said. She closed her eyes. I admired her beauty. "So, friends with benefits then?"

She reached down and guided me inside her. "Fuckin' A, drummer."

When I woke the next morning, I forced my eyes open with the help of the sun streaking through the blinds. Tracy's cute little face rested on my chest. She had a half smile on her lips.

"Good morning, rocker," she said, without opening her eyes.

"It is a good morning." With eyes still closed she craned her neck up to kiss me.

"You know I love your cute little ski-jump nose," I said.

"Really? Back in high school everyone thought I did cocaine cause o' the shape of this puppy. That and my energy."

"I can't imagine your energy back in the day. I bet it wasn't legal."

With a giggle, she popped up, tossed the comforter to the side and pulled me out of bed.

"Easy sister, what's this?"

"We're going to shower." She paused. "And you're going to like it."

"Who sent you?"

Tracy was on the nose with a thousand percent correctness. It was a shower I'm not likely to ever forget. I gathered my clothes off the floor. Tracy pulled various items from a distressed blond pine dresser.

"So, tell me about your drunk friend, the one from last night."

"Bobby? He's an acquaintance, at best, but to hear him tell it we're buds that go way back. Sometimes he tells girls we're cousins," I said, "if he thinks it'll help get him laid."

"He cornered me outside while you were packing up. Moose kept an eye on him while we shot the shit. It was kinda funny seeing him trying to eyeball Moose every two minutes."

"Oh my God. What'd Moose do?"

"Looked at him bored, as if trying to decide whether to throw a Fiat 500 at him."

I feared what was coming next. So I kept up the Moose talk.

"I once saw Moose slap a guy openhanded and knock him out."

"Really?" she chuckled.

"While he had another loser in a headlock," I said.

"That's the shit, so what happened next?"

"I don't know, I passed out from the headlock."

"Oh shit, are you serious?" she laughed.

"Nah, just playin'. I was on stage chucking sticks in between beats of Van Halen's "Hot for Teacher," which ain't easy, baby."

She fed me a sly grin with her hands on her hips.

"So, Bob's a bass player," she said with one eyebrow raised.

And there it was, the conversation I was trying to avoid.

"Wherever you're going, the answer is no. He's not reliable in the slightest—plays all right but—"

"I wanna try him out. I'm *going*—to try him out."

"Bad idea, hot stuff," I said, sliding my jeans on. "We have an expression in Canada for guys like Bobby."

"Oh?"

"Yes, Bob is what's called a 'fuck up'. Have you heard the term?"

Tracy grinned at me. "It's already done, the audition anyway."

I made a big deal of sighing heavily and ran a hand over my head. "The minute he pisses me off, he's out or no deal."

"Deal," she smiled.

"Good, he's out."

"What do you mean?"

"He just pissed me off, and I don't even know how. Just by being that guy—"

"You're being a bit of a bitch, Lou."

I grinned at her insane body. She knew she was a sexual dynamo. She fronted a great band, had a ton of talent and was sexually free, not to mention in control. Women in her position usually get a nasty name attached to them, yet when a guy does the same thing it's just another day at the office—another notch in the belt.

"You're lucky I'm a sucker for tough broads."

She didn't take her gaze off me as she shimmied into her panties. I was tempted to remove the jeans I'd just put on but wasn't sure how much reserves I had in the tank. She caught my look. She'd seen it many times long before she knew me, I was sure of it. Dang she was fine. She finally broke the stare and moved toward the closet and kicked a broken plastic laundry basket aside.

"Ah, what good is a laundry basket with no bottom to it? It's busted. What do you keep that for?"

"Apparently you've never seen an alien being born."

"Come again?"

"Soon, I'm sure. But for now, watch this."

She grabbed a T-shirt and pulled it over her head, then got down on the floor in front of the bottomless plastic laundry basket. Moving like an inchworm she wriggled toward the basket and squeezed into the hole. The entire time she shrieked like what I guessed was an alien. As she crawled through, her face popped through the T-shirt all twisted and distorted. It was one of the funniest things I'd ever seen.

"Voila," she said bouncing up with a laugh. "An alien birth."

"You are nuts," I said applauding her. She skipped toward me and jumped, landing with her legs around my waist. She kissed me deeply but to both of our surprise, I put the brakes on.

"Whoa!"

"What?"

"Whoa!"

"What the fuck, Crasher?"

"That move, the alien thing. Plus, Mrs. Wiggins buttered her toast with such a frail little wrist...and then there were the little booties at the Kensingtons." I kissed her hard and fast.

"What the hell are you—"

"The tent gang, you've heard of them, right?"

"Hell-to-the-duh, who hasn't, dummy?"

"They're small. They wore small-sized booties. There was a knife used to slice a tent and the handle was small, meaning the knife was small, which also suggests small hands. And...on one of the jobs one of the crew got in through a doggie door."

"And?"

"And your cute little alien-birthie thing. I bet you could fit through a doggie door, huh?"

"Hell yeah, doggie doors, heating ducts, cat doors—" she said proudly.

"Son of a—the tent gang are women! They're goddamn women!"

Tracy took a moment to take in my ramblings until finally, she said, "Nice, I think I love those scandalous bitches."

"I try not to use that word for—"

"Lose the pants Crasher, it's time you fucked this alien bitch—again."

CHAPTER FOURTEEN

Tracy had every intention of making me breakfast, but our last dance ran a little long and she had somewhere to be.

"I promise you a big fat breakfast next time," she said. It was all good with me. It was approaching eleven-thirty a.m. when Meredith called and asked if I had found out anything.

"On my way over," I told her.

When I reached her house, I slid in between a Volvo wagon and a Toyota Tacoma and locked my security steering wheel club into place.

"Come on in, Mr. Crasher," she said, turning and walking down the hall. I closed the door behind me. We sat in the same chairs as on my previous visit. I launched right into my visit to the college campus.

"Tyrone and Chicken, short for Chicken Little, cause he light skin-ded. Good boys. They came by to check on me," she said.

"They seem like good guys."

Her eyes took on a memory, then filled with tears. She took a handkerchief from her cardigan sleeve and dabbed at her eyes.

"Sorry, Mr. Crasher."

"Not at all. There'll be a lot o' that. Ya gotta just let it out."

She recovered quickly, folded her hands in her lap, then put her eyes on me—eyes that were equal parts grief and anger.

"The tent gang are women," I blurted. Her eyebrows went up,

then she rose from her seat and picked up a photo of Cody, running a hand across his image.

"Is that a fact, or a suspicion?"

"A theory," I said. "That I know in my bones to be true."

I ran the list of clues and finessed them into near facts. She nodded and sat back down with the photo on her lap.

"So what next?" she asked with eyes now empty of emotion.

"I've got a few ideas, starting with Jake. I've got something I need him to do, then I'll know which way to go from there."

I wasn't giving her much because I didn't have much, but I was confident I'd get there.

"I bet them bitches be white," she said, clenching a fist on the picture frame. Her jaw muscles contracted and her eyes narrowed. The statement seemed to echo off the walls and bounce from photo to photo. I waited until the reverb faded like a haunting Billie Holiday track.

"What makes you say that?" I asked, expecting a racist-fueled rant.

"Most o' them houses they rob be in nice neighborhoods, so if they go in early to case them places, like I 'spect they do, they'd raise all kinds o' suspicion if they be niggas or Mexicans." She hurled the words out as if spitting on the grave of an enemy.

"Fair point."

"How you think they move the stuff?" The question caught me off guard.

"Excuse me?"

"The crew. How you think them bitches move the property? Can't use a car, not enough room."

"They could use multiple cars, but more than likely a van or truck. They'd want to be together. Truck would have to be nice and have a shell on it. And a van, well, definitely couldn't be the creepy, no-window, abduct-a-toddler-type panel van."

"Minivan" she said.

"Like soccer moms take their kids to games in."

She managed the tiniest of smiles. "We gonna solve this shit yet, Mr. Crasher."

The solemnity returned to her face. Her eyes bore into mine. "Tell me, Mr. Crasher, who be drivin' soccer-mom minivans?"

I remained quiet, knowing where she was going.

"Well, if you won't say it, I will. White bitches—that who you be lookin' for. White bitches done kilt my boy!" she said, and pounded on the frame, causing the glass to crack.

I got up and moved to her. "Are you all right?"

"I'm fine. Don't touch me."

I held up my hands in surrender and sat back down. I considered leaving but remembered something.

"Why didn't you tell me about Cody's suspension? About the Adderall?"

Her eyes had aggravated assault in them. She clenched her teeth and spoke slowly. "Because it don't have a damn thing to do with why he got shot, that's why."

"You should let me decide what's relevant, Meredith. It's how I work cases."

"Cases, ha!" she said, rolling her eyes.

"I'm on your side, Meredith. Maybe you didn't ask for my help, but Jake did and until he pulls me off—"

She stood, slammed the photo on the table, destroying what was left of the frame.

"I need to look after this," she said, holding up her bleeding hand, and shuffled to the kitchen. I let myself out.

Jake was leaning on my Mustang with arms folded and one foot crossed over the other when I came out. He wore a short-sleeve black T-shirt and jeans.

"You rode today," I said, noticing his motorcycle boots. He gave me a short nod. His bike must have been down the block. I gave him the most abridged version of events. He listened while staring straight ahead as if counting roof tiles on Meredith's house.

"What do you need from me?"

"I need to know what the cops know. They always sit on info then just sprinkle out crumbs to the media. What are they sitting on?"

"Already done." That was really why he was there.

"Go on."

"I've got a guy with ears. It's believed the crew is a three-man team."

"Women."

"I'm giving you what I've got, you want it or not?" It was my turn to give him a short nod.

"They don't use their real names. Cocktail names: Moscow Mule, Boilermaker and I.P.A."

"Huh, sounds like—"

"If you crack wise it'll be injurious for you."

I buttoned my lip. He hauled his phone out and punched something in. My phone vibrated a second later.

"That's the most recent address on Moscow Mule. I recommend checking him out."

"Her. And thanks."

My "thanks" was to his V-shaped back moving away. I climbed into my ride and put Moscow Mule's address into the Maps App. Once I had a route locked in, I heard Jake's Ducati roar up in the distance. I woke up the ol' gal in response.

CHAPTER FIFTEEN

Moscow Mule lived in West Hollywood, not far from Beverly Hills. I was looking at just under three million bucks if I'd had my checkbook with me and wanted to buy the place. It was a white Spanish revival number with black window frames. The smooth stucco is popular these days, but rumors claim it invites cracks in a town that sits on a serious earthquake fault line. This seemed off. The property would suggest Moscow Mule is wealthy. There's no way the house was paid for from robbing eight houses split three ways. Maybe she was into other things, or maybe up to this point she'd been a safe- cracker or diamond thief. Maybe grandma had left the joint to her; too many maybes. I rechecked the text from Jake, the address was correct, unless his guy with ears got it wrong.

I got out for a closer look. I was confident she didn't know who I was, so I wasn't worried about being made. I walked across the street and stopped in front of the house. I faked looking at something on my phone while spying on the place out of the corner of my eye. I continued along the sidewalk. Glancing down a side walkway, I noticed a large guesthouse at the back of the property. That could be where she lays her head, I told myself. I walked halfway down the block, crossed the street and headed back to the ol' gal. The stars aligned thirty minutes later when a woman decked out head to toe in an aquamarine-blue Nike fitness suit emerged from the side of the house. A blond ponytail poked out of the back of a Nike baseball cap. She moved quickly down the walk and climbed into a four-year-old Honda Civic. I held up my phone, partially covering my face. When she pulled onto the street, I brought my ride to life, pulled a U-turn and followed her.

Moscow Mule never signaled her turns and ran all yellow lights, causing me to accelerate through reds. She pulled into a 24-Hour Fitness lot, parked, and jogged to the gym. I put her at no taller than five-two. Her toned body could be seen through her fitness gear. I thought back to Tracy's alien birth routine and had no problem envisioning Moscow Mule squeezing through a doggie door to relieve people of their possessions.

Twenty minutes into her workout I bought two tacos from Gigi's Food Truck.

"Tres dollores."

"Only three bucks? Nice. Mucho gracias, amigo," I said.

"De nada."

I chased the tacos down with water. They hit the spot. Forty minutes later the tent thief came out of the door. An Asian gent in a charcoal tracksuit was walking behind her and seemed annoyed that Moscow Mule hadn't held the door for him. She skipped down the steps with ponytail bouncing behind her. I tailed her.

An hour later she was home, showered and heading back out again.

Where to, Ms. Mule?

She took the most direct route to a modern three-story condo in the Los Feliz area. Before approaching the building, she checked up and down the sidewalk. As she moved toward the building she no longer walked with the confident "I got this" fitness gait. She seemed almost tentative. I wondered if she was casing the joint until she raised her hand to the buzzer panel. I took a quick shot with my cell. Even with the zoom I couldn't get the number, but I was able to see that she buzzed one of the top two numbers on the panel.

She turned her back to the door as she waited and looked around nervously. Whoever she buzzed was expecting her because Moscow Mule never announced herself; she just entered once the door clicked. I was already out of the ol' gal and watching from behind a raised Chevy pickup with oversized tires. When the door closed behind her, I took the steps two at a time. I hoped for a name—no such luck, just numbers. Her party was either in unit one or unit two. As I was about to leave, something caught my attention on the panel. With a closer look I realized it was a tiny camera lens. And I looked smack-dab in the middle of it—a truly amateur move. Hoping Moscow Mule's party was no longer watching wasn't going to cut it. I had to fix my mistake. I buzzed number seven.

"Yeah?" A male voice answered, sounding impatient.

"It's Johnny Walker Black," I said. "I'm a Jehovah's witness."

"Fuck off."

"Jehovah loves you. Have yourself a blessed day."

I hope that did it. My phone buzzed as I opened my car door.

"This is Lou Crasher."

"Hey Crasher, it's Shawn Kensington. You were here looking into—"

"Uh-huh I remember, what's up?"

"Got something for ya. You need to get over here."

"A pic won't do?"

"No, this is a little thing called evidence, pal."

I decided to let Moscow chill. I figured they wouldn't be hitting any houses until the wee hours of night or early morning. I could pick her up again at her crib. At least now I had two addresses. I figured Jim Rockford would agree with the play, although Jimmy would never have looked into that camera lens like I did.

CHAPTER SIXTEEN

Shawn Kensington was in his front yard pulling weeds when I rolled up. He dusted his hands off on his black jeans before shaking my hand. He was shirtless and made a point of quick-twitch-flexing his muscles. The show went pecs, biceps, triceps and back to pecs.

The wag of the dog's tail.

"Thanks for coming Crasher. Say, can I call you Crash?"

"Why not, it's what the guys call me down at the lodge."

"Good. Follow me."

As we walked to the right side of his house, he told me he was the nickname king. He claimed he had coined *The Rattle Snake* for wrestler Stone Cold Steve Austin. This was why he needed to call me Crash.

"Really? The Rattle Snake?" I asked, knowing he was bullshitting me.

"More or less," he said.

A wooden gate led down a narrow walk between his place and the neighbor's. We held up halfway down the walk.

"Check it out," he said, pulling a blue tarp off a dead possum carcass. "Nasty little fucker, huh Crash?"

"I can't say what his personality was like. Never met him before. I hope this isn't why you—"

"Nah, it was under the house in the crawl space. I smelled

something awful in the house and this is what it turned out to be. Anyway, while I'm down there I find this shit."

He reached into the crawl space and pulled out a clear plastic bag. Inside it was a spray can.

"Hmm. I take it the color matches the graffiti on your fridge?"

"You catch on quick, Crash. Shit, Quick Crash would be a dope wrestling name, bro."

"No doubt. May I take this?"

"It's why you're here."

"I'm sure the prints are scrubbed but maybe the brand is rare, and I can run it down."

"Like I said. It's why you're here, Crash." He slapped me hard on the back intentionally as in "we're buddies but feel my power." I fed him dead eyes, which had him yank his hand back as if my shoulder were fire-poker hot.

Kensington wouldn't let me leave with the spray can until I promised to give him any info I found before I went to the cops. He said I'd be a shit-prick if I broke my promise. When I gave him the necessary assurances, he smiled wide-eyed. This was truly more fun for him than writing wrestling stories.

Before heading home, I swung by Earl's Hardware Store. They weren't the biggest of the box stores, but some claimed they were better.

"Welcome to Earl's. My name is Janice, just like the tag says. How can I help the man with the pretty eyes?"

I thanked her for the compliment then showed her the picture of the spray can on my phone.

"I'm hoping you'll tell me this brand is rare."

"Best not to lose hope," she said stepping through the saloon-style door.

"Bring those eyes this way."

We walked down an aisle then took two lefts and a right. The spray cans were locked in a cage with a massive padlock on it.

That's Los Angeles for you. One column from floor to ceiling, the height of the Empire State building, carried the brand I was looking for.

"Aw, nuts."

"Normally customers sigh with relief when we carry what they ask for. Why'd you want this to be rare?" Janice asked.

"I'm working something."

"Thank God that's not vague."

"Sorry, working a case and was hoping I could track somebody with this."

"Sounds like somebody should have managed his expectations," she said. "Ever considered meditation?" A few strands of hair fell from her ponytail, which she gently tucked behind her ear.

"You're a cheeky little thing, aren't you, Janice?"

She pulled a business card from the back pocket of her tight bell-bottom jeans and handed it to me. It bore the company logo, but it was her personal card. It also read, "Manager."

"I'd say I don't normally do this but that'd be a lie, and if that scares you, well, then it's been fun," she smiled. "But not as much fun as it will be if you call."

"Only time I've been scared was the day I was born."

"Oh?"

"Yeah, when the doc delivered me and spanked me, and I was scared I was going to kill him right there in the O.R."

She stepped close and looked up at me. She smelled of vanilla and good times.

"What happens next is up to you, Pretty Eyes." And with that she walked back to the counter. As she entered the saloon doors, she gave me a look full of promises and naughty intentions.

I was almost home and running down my sandwich and beer options when I got a call. It was Susie from work. Susie's priorities were: party hard, show up for work, sometimes party harder, repeat.

This ought to be rich.

"What's up, girl?"

"I just wanted to say sorry about being such a dick lately—not really the coolest welcome to the new manager."

"Thanks, doll, I dig you calling with this. So what do you need?"

"Geez, what makes you think—can't a girl apologize?"

"Yes, sorry. And thank you."

"So—"

Here it comes...

"I was wondering if you could throw me a couple of extra shifts. My indulgences have really kicked me in the C-word."

"And by 'C' I hope you mean cash flow. But this is perfect. How 'bout tonight? Take my shift."

I heard her say 'shit' under her breath.

"Aha, careful what you ask for, baby doll."

"Fuck me, okay, I'll do it. I need the dough."

"So you said. Six till close. I'd owe you one, but managers never owe, especially the good-looking ones."

"You're such a jerk," she laughed, "by the way, you deserve it, the manager gig."

"Gracias to that."

"Ain't no surprise the way you kiss up to Pops Carruthers all the time," she laughed.

"I've never kissed up to—"

The phone beeped, signaling she'd killed the call. With the shift covered I was all set for late-night Moscow Mule surveillance. But first it was home for a sandwich and a couple beers. Tonight's menu would be my classic S.S. tuna melt. It sounds like the name of a ship but it's not.

I opened the fridge and began an inventory check. Celery, red onion, twelve-grain bread, sharp cheddar, butter, black pepper, canned tuna, hot mustard, chili flakes and Booker's bourbon. That covered the S.S. tuna melt. Accompanying beers would be

Kirin, a Korean delight. The S.S. actually stands for *spicy-sexy*, not a ship reference.

I first made the sandwich for a delectable bass player from the Philippines who showed her gratitude in ways I couldn't begin to count. *She* was drop-dead sexy, and the chili flakes cover the spicy part.

I started by dicing the red onion, because once diced it needs to soak in the Booker's bourbon, which is a smooth but gritty spirit recommended by Moose, the bouncer over at Club Zoot Suit. I downed half a Kirin while getting everything else ready. I fried the onions in butter and added a splash of Booker's and lit it on fire. This move isn't necessary, but fire is, well, cool. Both sides of the bread buttered, mayo and mustard in place. Next came the tuna, sharp cheddar, boozy onions, then the flakes. With a second pan heated just right, I laid the treat down with care. I killed the other half of the beer and opened a second. After a quick peek with the spatula I saw that the sandwich wasn't ready to turn. I did a quick twenty-five pushups, checked again, and turned the creation with more care than the crew leader of a bomb squad cutting the red wire.

The sandwich was a gorgeous golden brown. I considered taking a photo but it's something I never do, ever. Three minutes later the creation is a masterpiece. A third Kirin acted as a palate-cleansing digestif. I took a catnap then showered.

It was eleven-thirty when I was behind the wheel of the ol' gal. She cranked up with a cough then roared to life. Twenty minutes later I sat outside Moscow Mule's. Burglary house number ten is two houses away for the tent gang. I wondered if tonight would be house nine. The media have blasted non-stop on the magic number ten from every loud hailer they've got. No doubt the tent gang are spurred on by the challenge. Any thrill-seeking media headline junkie would be. This may cause them to make a mistake, which might help me wrap them up in my dragnet. The scenario will help bring peace to Meredith Billups.

The stakeout is a miserable affair. I cursed myself for having that third beer. I risked being made by hopping out of the ride and relieving myself in a nearby hedge. By two-thirty-three a.m. my head was doing the head bob shuffle, fighting sleep. Ten minutes after that I was about to crank the engine over when Moscow Mule emerged from the side of the big house. I almost missed her due to her dark garb. My heart rate ticked up immediately. I slumped low in my seat. She walked to her Honda but then continued past. She had passed three cars when I got out, gently eased my door closed with my hip and trotted down the sidewalk on the opposite side of the street. Where the hell was she going? Moscow rounded the corner. I put my legs in high gear to catch up. When I got to the intersection, I saw her climb into a non-descript, plain-Jane, soccer-mom minivan.

Son of a bitch, Billups called it...

I spun on a rock 'n' roll dime and horsed it back to my ride—she cranked up on the first try. I punched it and hurried down the block. At the intersection I saw her brake lights disappear around a left turn. She rounded another corner but by then I had caught up to a safe tailing distance. On the main streets I moved up closer only one of two lanes over from her. After another five miles or so she drove into Century City. We wound through a half-dozen residential streets until she pulled to a curb at a fire hydrant. She wasn't staying long. Both brake and cell phone lights glowed. I killed my headlights. In under a minute two dark-clad figures quick-walked down the steps of a five-story apartment building called the Sea Star and climbed into the van. I put them all around Moscow Mule's height. Small—petit even. Women.

I was not only looking at the tent gang I was about to shadow them to robbery house number nine. And at least one of them could be Cody's killer. I heard a thumping in my ears and realized it was my heartbeat.

I kept my lights off during the neighborhood trek back to the main streets then I pulled the lights up and held way back, seeing as traffic was almost non-existent. We made our way back to

Sunset Boulevard where we moved east all the way to the Pacific Palisades, another neighborhood I'd likely never call home unless Yesterday's Pop Tart landed a huge record deal…and even then…

They pulled down Napoli Drive. When I got to the corner and made the turn, a private neighborhood security guard was parked thirty feet back from Sunset. The minivan was halfway down the block, home free. They passed the smell test, my ride wouldn't. A brother in a beat-up classic ride rolling through the Palisades at that hour would have some explaining to do. It isn't right but that's where we are. The guard's eyes grew to baseball size when he locked onto me. I decided to take the conflict to him.

I pulled level with his car and stopped. We rolled windows down at the same time, only mine took longer seeing as it was an old-school manual hand crank.

"Excuse me?"

"Yes?" His eyes were hard beneath a creased brow and had the weariness of a lengthy work shift behind them.

"I'm headed back to Hollywood but need to gas up. Where would the closest station be that's still open?"

"Back to Sunset, hang a right and it's about three blocks down. It's open all night, but the store is closed so if you want any grub ya gotta go to the security window."

"Thanks pal, I appreciate it. Say, what time is your shift done?" I say, friendly.

"Fuckin' six."

"Grindin' huh?"

"Ain't nobody payin' my bills but me."

"I get it. I did security up in Seattle," I lied. "Same gig, different shitty city."

"Bet you don't miss the rain, huh?" he said.

"Hell no," I said sliding my shifter into drive. "Will this road let me out so I don't have to three-point-turn this old girl?"

"Yeah, bro."

"Thanks."

I rolled away in search of the crew. I wasn't too worried, seeing as all I had to do was find the big fat circus tent around a mansion with a minivan within reach. I had the house in under five minutes. I hauled my phone and readied to call the law once the crew scrambled out. A minute that seemed like five crawled by. Screw it, I thought and decided to creep up close and verify. I'd get close, see them in the act and come back out and make my call—no need to wait for them to come out. Who knew how long the cops might take to show. I killed the engine and rolled the window up. I stepped out and heard a buzzing sound behind me and knew immediately that it wasn't a colony of bees passing by. It was an amateur move, not checking my rearview or side mirrors before stepping out.

My body was suddenly slammed with fifty thousand volts of electricity.

Taser. Fuck.

I went down to a knee with one hand on the driver's door and turned toward my attacker. He grabbed my wrist as if to twist my arm behind my back. I jerked away from the hold and ended up on my back. A blurred-out face peering from inside a hood looked down at me. The taser came in for another zap. Upon contact I managed to bat it away. It was a fluke but even flukes count. I heard the weapon slide across the pavement. I willed myself to get up and fight, but the legs weren't ready. A combat boot with a zig-zag tread hovered above my head. I raised my forearm in defense but was eons too late. The boot came down hard. I saw a flash of white before the black swarm of horse flies seeped in from the edges of my vision. I'm assuming I went out at that point.

CHAPTER SEVENTEEN

The stars above were bright but not outdoor-camping-in-the-country bright. The distant traffic sound was sporadic. I rolled to my side, then pushed up to a sitting position. Being as I had been tased on the street, my attacker had dragged me up over the curb and onto the damp grass. A courteous move, but it meant my assailant, although small in size, had been strong enough to drag two hundred and twelve pounds of slumbering rock drummer to comfy climbs. I checked the house while wiping the blurriness from my eyes. The mansion was still enveloped in the tent, but the van was nowhere in sight. As I gingerly touched the swollen lump on my cheek, a voice in my skull told me I should have called the law the minute I arrived at the house and saw the van. Jake might throw me off a building when he hears of the blunder. Hindsight and wallowing weren't going to make my semi-concussion go away so why swim in the above-ground self-pity pool?

Recalling a show on *Dateline* about tasers, I checked my crotch. Dry. Thank God I hadn't pissed myself like many taser victims do. I got to my knees and checked the passenger door. Locked. I used the handle to pull myself upright. My legs made me feel like I was moving up a down escalator. I hugged the ride as I rounded to the driver's door, which my attacker had closed but left unlocked. I clambered in and checked my phone. I'd been out eight minutes. Having been boot-stomped before, I knew eight minutes was way too long for me to be out; must have been the addition of the electric jolt.

I replayed the event as best I could before cranking up my ride. I ran the play forward and backward and cringed each time I got to the point of the buzzing zapper. A blurry vision kept appearing and disappearing. It was there, then gone, over and over. Focus, Crasher. The pinholes for eyes had looked almost black and deep set within the hoodie. *It wasn't that, though; get off that, Crasher.* I shook my head to clear the cobwebs and nearly screamed in pain. All that did was rattle my brain and sting like a migraine. But then the image appeared as if out of smoke and fog: a tattoo! Yes!

When I had knocked the taser from the assailant's hand, the cuff of the thick sweatshirt slid up the veiny forearm, revealing a tattoo on the inside wrist. I scrambled for a pen and paper from my glove compartment and began sketching out the picture. I lay the crude drawing on the passenger seat, stared at my work, and thought about the wrist bearing the tat. It was skinny but not slender. More like lean, bluish veins, no forearm hair...a woman's.

Son of a...

CHAPTER EIGHTEEN

Julie "Trusty Lesbo" McCall sat at her laptop in a kimono adorned with images of battling samurai warriors. She was doing a deep dive into the man she had tased an hour earlier. With the use of his license plate she had obtained more than enough to stroll through the drummer's life—a drummer whose occasional meddling had landed him in the headlines of small publications, often as a local mini-hero.

She pulled her foot up on the chair and hugged her knee as she moved the cursor around the screen. Crasher was sticking his nose into the tent gang's business—but why? Trusty had followed her crew around to all of their jobs from day one. The crew was clueless as to her presence. They never knew she was there inside the houses with them. The closest they had come to detecting her was the occasional pause in movement by Moscow Mule. Moscow had a sixth sense, for sure, but hadn't fine-tuned it enough to catch Trusty in the houses with them or spot her when she tailed them through the streets.

Lou Crasher's tailing of the crew was an entertaining distraction to her routine—tailing the tail. She was impressed that he had gotten past the rent-a-cop, because there was no chance he'd gotten into that neighborhood without showing I.D. and staring down the barrel of a Maglite at the very least—rent-a-cops were the worst.

So why was he interfering? Just chasing another headline? Trusty looked to the historical and found that Crasher had been mixed up in a case involving a priceless vintage snare drum and came out smelling like a rose. A check to see if he had a P.I.'s license proved negative.

"You Boy Scout, good Samaritan, wannabe hero, fuck wad," she whispered.

She cast the net wider and checked out his social. "Ooh, those bitches are hot," she thought as she dug up info on two martial art gym owners, Katherine and Tamika. One was black and the other Asian. *Y'all are some fine breezy bitches.* She wondered if Crasher was boning one or both of them; they all seemed close. And that meant she'd just found the drummer's Achilles heel. She closed the laptop, sipped her rum and thought about how she was going to hit Crasher where it hurt.

A grin crossed her face. She opened the computer again and briefly zoomed in on a photo of the martial artists. *Dang.*

She finished her rum, placed the mug beside the laptop and padded barefoot to the bedroom. She opened her bedside table drawer and pulled out her Gasm XTC 500 clitoral stimulator and powered it up. She lay back, closed her eyes and put herself in a room with the black chick and the Asian. With the fantasy set, she let the toy work its magic.

CHAPTER NINETEEN

Moscow Mule didn't feel right. Something was wrong but she couldn't nail it down. It was becoming a problem. Her chest would tighten for no known reason. When she was young, she had had a heart issue for which she underwent minor surgery, but that had cleared everything up. It couldn't be that, could it? It must be anxiety, she thought. It must be the kid. Had Trusty killed him? Was she a killer? It scared her how little she knew about the creepy hacker. And if not Trusty, then who? What a fucking nightmare.

Maybe it was the stress of the tenth and last job coming up. It shouldn't be; it's just another house to the gang. But the whole crew was on edge, and it was her job to settle the restless herd.

She looked over the haul from the first nine jobs. Most of it had been divvied up, but not all. It was time to dole out some more. Women like gifts. Maybe this would help ease the tension, she thought. But it would be only a Band-Aid because Moscow Mule could feel that something bad was coming. Someone was watching her; she could sense it. And that was problematic because she had a goal. It was all about the goal, and nothing could stand in the way: not her nervous crew, not Trusty possibly going rogue, or whatever thing was out there haunting her. She considered postponing the tenth job—maybe. She'd talked about the crew moving in another direction. Maybe quitting while they were ahead was the way to go.

She bent down and picked up a pair of Jimmy Choos patent leather sandals, which I.P.A. would love, and a pair of Miu Miu ankle boots that Boilermaker would flip over. She backed out of the room and locked the door. "Fucking tenth house. Keep your eye on the prize, bitch," she mumbled before stalking down the hall. The goal was all that mattered, but for now, she had a pep talk to deliver.

CHAPTER TWENTY

The weather app on my phone claimed I had awakened to eighty degrees and slight winds. Chance of rain was two percent, so why mention it? I lazed around most of the morning. drinking tons of water. By noon I was at my drum lockout laying down grooves and letting the mind float.

I was fifteen minutes late letting progressive rock band Salted Pork into their practice room at the Joint. They were none too happy and called the shop, which forwarded the call to Eddie Carruthers at his home.

"Not what I was expecting from my newly minted manager, Lou."

"I know, Big Eddie, I'm sorry. I had a bizarre case thing go down last night."

"Oh, I see. Ya wanna make sure you can strike a balance between jobs Lou, cause—"

"Couldn't agree more. This won't happen again." Even as I said it, I had trouble believing my words.

With the exception of the joyful hour I got to play with reggae band Sugar Cane Riddim, whose drummer was late, my shift was uneventful. When it was over, I hopped into the ol' gal and pointed her south on La Brea toward Melrose Avenue. I hung a right on Melrose and two and a half blocks later parked in front of Sick Tattoo and entered the parlor.

"What's up?" the counterman asked. Both arms were covered in tattoos. The look is referred to as *sleeves*. He had six visible piercings, one of which was in his nose. His thin black hair struggled in length to form the world's tiniest man-bun. He did his best to pretend I didn't have a reddish-purple bruise on my cheek. I laid out my sketch of the tattoo I'd drawn on the counter.

"Seen anything like this before?"

He gingerly folded a corner of the paper down and squinted at the image. He then backed away as if the paper contained traces of the Corona virus.

"Yo, Ni," he called without taking his gaze off the sheet. "Nima? Out front, please."

A woman that I'm sure is often mistaken for Mexican but is more likely Iranian entered through hanging beads that separated the front room from the back. She had as many tats as Man Bun and moved straight to the counter.

"My guess is you got the better of the other guy," she said, looking at my face.

"You're too kind. And yes, let's go with your version."

With a warm smile she moved her eyes to the sketch, then glowered. Barely above a whisper she told Man Bun she'd handle it. He took the cue and strolled to the back. She finally put eyes on me.

"Are you wanting this as a tattoo?"

"Not in the slightest."

"Where did you see this?"

"A woman on the other side of fifty thousand volts had it on her arm."

She let out a sigh. "What do you think it signifies?"

"That's why I came to you, but to me it's a dagger sunk three-quarters deep into a human skull. Any heavy metal kid would don this, but it's the letters that throw me off."

"We'll get to those in a minute," she said. "What do you think about the way the skull is grinning?"

"It's lopsided like the tattoo artist was knee-deep in the cinnamon bourbon when she worked on it."

"Actually, it's by design, to distinguish it from a regular skull tattoo. Do you see the striations on the knife handle?"

"Yeah, like the leather grip as it wraps around."

"Yes, but in this case, it signifies rank. The more striations, the—"

"Higher the rank."

"Yes."

"Ranking in what?" I asked.

"Coming to that. You wondered about the letters."

She spun my drawing back around so I could read it. The letters started on one side of the skull, moved over the top of the knife handle then came down to the other side of the skull.

"Yes, H.C.E.T. what—"

"What if I told you to read it backwards?"

"T-E—tech."

"Correct, this person is part of tech, a hacker."

"Okay, I get that, but you said there was a ranking."

"This hacker belongs to an underground anarchist group called *Disruptor*."

"Not very imaginative."

"Agreed. Do you have a few more minutes?"

I told her yes and she called Man Bun back to watch the front. We did a quick formal introduction where Man Bun did his best to avoid eye contact before she and I went through the beads to the back room.

"Sit there," Nima said, pointing me to a stool similar to my drum throne. She opened a mini-fridge and pulled out a bottle of booze and two chilled tumblers.

"Ah, you're a fan."

"Why am I drooling?" I asked.

"Like a basset hound. Neat or rocks, Mr. Crasher?"

"You can call me Lou if you like. And one rock will be divine."

Before handing me my drink she wrapped each in a double napkin. We clinked glasses and took pulls. Her thick black hair was pulled back. One of her eyebrows had a break in it, as if she'd taken a knife wound and the hair hadn't grown back. Her sharp blue eyes radiated from olive skin. She seemed to be studying me. After a second sip she put the tumbler on the table next to her. I told her how much I adored Booker's bourbon and she smiled like we were day-players on a film set.

"If you were tased then you are marked on their radar. And you have my sympathies."

"What else do you know about them?"

"They are anarchist rabble-rousers. They protest, they're into corporate espionage, they beat, steal, maim, you name it. They—"

"Disrupt," I said. With a nod, she picked up her drink. I took another swig as well. The sauce soothed going down, but the back of my neck heated it up the way it does when my anger rises. I don't like being threatened or sitting in a petri dish under the microscope of some misguided fanatical group. I fought the rage, which can cause me not to think straight.

"What about the hacker? Why would she be out tasing people? I thought hackers sat in basements in front of computers and ruined people's lives, one click at a time." I said. "Not that there are many basements in L.A. but—" I trailed off.

Nima pulled her thick brown hair around in a sort of practiced twist maneuver and popped it up into a bun. My look conveyed that I thought the move was sexy and she caught it with a mini-smile.

"You remember how many striations on the knife? She is high-ranking. She's a hacker but I believe she's many other things as well."

I killed the rest of the booze and rose to leave.

"You should go out the back, Lou, in case you were tailed here."

I nodded. "Thank you for the info, Nima," I said, folding the sketch and putting it in my jeans pocket.

"Your eyes tell me that you'll try and get the jump on her. I warn you that she'll be dangerous and even if you take her out,

Disruptor's membership runs deep and wide."

"I'll cross Disruptor's bridge when I—"

"Then I wish you happy hunting, Lou Crasher," she said, cutting off my false bravado. I handed her my card and asked her to call if she thought of anything else.

"My father was a drummer," she said, running a finger across the card.

"Then I'm sure he was a good man. Thanks again for the sweet elixir," I paused at the door. We held each other's look. She studied. I digested.

"I dig the chilled tumblers. Gonna try that."

CHAPTER TWENTY-ONE

Kat stood in the center of the octagonal-shaped mixed-martial-arts ring known as the octagon and watched the five youths, three boys and two girls, jog the perimeter.

"Come on, guys, keep it up, let's go. If your opponent is an even-fight match, the kid in better shape wins. Push it, push it!" She adjusted the padded kicking bag she held and stood ready.

"Alfred, you're up. Roundhouse kicks on me, right leg then left leg. Hustle up. The rest of you keep jogging."

The pudgy ten-year-old jogged over to Kat, put his hands on his knees and bent over.

"Oh no you don't, come on Alfred, give me two, you can do it."

The boy struggled but complied. Kat noticed his technique was still a mess, but the kid had power.

"Wow, did you hear that, kids? Alfred is bringin' H-E-A-T today. Listen to that pop. Two more, come on. Let's rotate that hip now, bring it."

Alfred put all he had into the kicks. Kat eased back slightly, absorbing the shock.

"Yes!" she said, and ruffled Alfred's hair, causing him to blush. "Hold!"

The kids stopped jogging. Kat looked at each one individually. The kids were being bullied at school, and that's why they were in Kat and Tami's gym; they wanted the bullying to stop. Kat was going to give them more than a fighting chance.

"Drop and give me twenty-five push-ups. Take the break if you need to, but get 'em done, all twenty-five. If you can do more go for it, but you better not do less, let's go!"

With groans and mumbles the kids got down to work. As Kat exited the cage two men and a woman came through the back door. Kat didn't like the look.

"We're just finishing up a private class and then we're closing. Sorry."

Only she wasn't sorry because she knew they weren't there to sign up. Her only thought was protecting the kids.

"Well, now that's not very hospitable," the tallest man said. He was scrawny with thin, greasy hair and horrible teeth.

A tweaker...

Kat walked up to the ringleader. "I don't know what you think is going to happen here, but I need you guys outta here—now."

The female of the group had wild eyes. She looked beyond Kat to the kids in the cage.

"Eyes on me, Sistah," Kat threatened through gritted teeth.

The medium-build Latino with bloodshot eyes looked like he didn't know what was happening. Kat worried about him the least. The tall one slowly pulled a .38-caliber snub- nose from his waistband and held it at his side.

"Let's say we head to the office and relieve you of some funds."

"This is a gym, and we've barely been open six months. How much you think you're gonna get, you idiot?"

"Let's go," the ringleader said, "before one of those fat fuckers in the cage gets hurt."

Kat desperately wanted to break his neck but couldn't risk the kids'.

"Follow me, assholes."

Kat led them to the office. The tall one kept his distance. He never got within three feet of her. Smart, she thought. She opened her desk drawer, pulled out an envelope and handed it to the woman. She tore at it like it was crystal meth, which it probably would become within five minutes of their leaving.

"Nice," the tweaker woman hissed.

"Ya see, bitch, that wasn't so hard, was it? You have a gorgeous day," the tall one said. Even from three feet his foul breath nearly knocked Kat back into the office chair.

They walked out and Kat let them go. After a quick check on the kids she told them to stay put and hauled out her phone. Tami was downtown, so no sense calling her. Lou!

CHAPTER TWENTY-TWO

I was on my way to my lockout to sit behind my drum kit and work through the case when my phone buzzed. I stuck it in the visor and hit the speaker option.

"Hey Kat, what's—"

"We just got robbed—gun point. I'm so *effing* pissed."

"Ah shit, are you hurt?"

"No, we're good."

"You and Tami?"

"Me and my anti-bullying students."

"You call the—"

"You know what, uh-uh. I ain't goin' out like this. I need that money. I'm gettin' it back."

"Kat don't you—you call the law right now. Don't be a—"

I got the three beeps of rejection. Kat and Tami's gym was in North Hollywood, which was where I was, in a neighborhood known as Valley Glen, just east of the 170 Freeway. I pinned the accelerator because I know Kat: She was going to finish what the robbers had started. She's not the victim type. I wasn't far from the gym. The gods were smiling because I caught green light after green light, which meant I never got a red light, which would have given me time to call the boys in blue. I was pretty sure they'd pop me soon anyway, the way I was driving. So be it, I'd lead them straight to the gym.

Two more blocks and I'd be off the main drag and into the warehouse area where the gym sits. Once in there I'd have no speed limit, and I could push the ol' gal to the brink. The final light was red. I ran it and narrowly missed a stretched-out motor home. The driver was forced to lock up his brakes and give me the middle finger for the effort. I came in hot to the right turn off Kline Street. A baker's dozen of cyclists were immediately in front of me, taking up the entire lane plus a portion of the oncoming lane. I honked while trying to swing out wide. My passenger side mirror clipped the outside rider. He lost it and took down three bikers with him.

"Sorry," I shouted out my window. I got more middle fingers and have no doubt that at least one of them got my license plate. Oh well.

I had a turn at every block and my tires sang their screechy song at each corner. I finally got myself a stretch of straightaway road.

"Hang on, girl, we're almost there. Gotta horse it now though." I floored it. The Mustang jumped. What a doll!

CHAPTER TWENTY-THREE

Kat could feel the nervousness of the kids. She did her best to calm them down and made them promise to stay inside. Meanwhile, she grabbed the brick that was used to keep the storeroom door open and jogged to the alley since the tweakers came in the back. She found them in a piece-of-shit Kia Soul with mismatching doors and no front hood. They were getting high and laughing. Kat marched straight up to the driver's door and smashed the window with the brick. The tall one screamed as glass showered over him. She gave him a straight right to the jaw, stunning him. She could have knocked him out but then he'd be dead weight. She wanted him light as she dragged him through the window and dumped him on the pavement.

"No, please," he whined.

Kat kicked him in the nuts then searched for the gun. It wasn't on him.

Shit...

The stoned-out girl got one leg out of the back door on the driver's side. Kat side-kicked the door closed and pinned it on the woman's shin. She howled. Kat released then reloaded and kicked again, knowing full well that the second kick snapped the shinbone clean through.

The out-of-it Latino popped up from the passenger front seat and began firing over the roof of the car. Kat ducked, hitting the pavement with a somersault to the car. She heard his footsteps rounding the front of the vehicle. She popped to a squat and did a fast sort of duck walk to the rear of the car.

I'm fucked...

"You think you can outrun bullets, bitch?" he taunted. As he came around the car Kat moved to the other side. She popped up to draw fire. He fired twice but missed as Kat dove into a shoulder roll to the front of the car. The girl with the busted leg toppled out of the vehicle and continued to howl. Just then, Alfred, one of Kat's students, came out of the gym's back exit with a pair of nunchuks. Kat tried to wave him away. The Latino spotted Alfred and fired a shot at him. Alfred ducked back inside as the bullet slammed into the steel door inches from where his head had been.

Kat went ballistic inside but couldn't risk rushing the shooter. A slow grin crossed her lips as she heard a car approach. She'd never been happier to see Lou's Mustang coming in hot...maybe too hot.

CHAPTER TWENTY-FOUR

As I rounded the last corner after the straightaway my back end kicked out. I eased up on the gas, corrected the skid, then put the pedal to the floor. Through dumb luck I saw a car and moving figures out of the corner of my eye in the alley behind the gym. I locked up the brakes, causing the rear driver's side to skid to the left. I slammed it in reverse and hugged the turn down the alley, gunning it in reverse—no time for the brake lockup, reverse, then forward. I've always been good at horsing it in reverse, ever since my unhinged uncle Curtis taught me with not-so-gentle shovel punches to the ribs whenever I veered off course. Out the back window I saw someone angling for a shot over the roof of a beat-up Kia. The alley was wide, as they tend to be in warehouse districts, for big cargo trucks. This meant I could take him where he stood, provided Kat kept him on his driver's side of the Kia. Some kid, probably one of Kat's students, came out of the gym's back exit, tossed something to Kat, and ducked back inside. Kat stretched a leg out and pulled what turned out to be nunchuks close. She popped up and hurled them at the shooter. He and the gun got tangled up in the chain between the wooden attack pieces. It was enough to distract him. He didn't even look my way when I shoved the ol' gal's rearend into his legs. He slammed onto my trunk, rolled over my roof, then bounced off the hood to the pavement. I locked up my brakes and hopped out. The gun slid away. Kat picked it up.

A woman was rolling around on the ground, screaming for help. Her foot and ankle appeared to almost dangle like a lonely yo-yo from her shinbone. The nunchuk-throwing kid ran to Kat and hugged her around the waist. As she congratulated him for his bravery, a skinny bastard struggled to his feet and ran for my Mustang, which was still idling. I grabbed him by the back of his collar and yanked hard, as if shaking dust off a rug, and hauled him all the way down to the ground, ensuring his spine from skull to coccyx made brutal contact with the pavement. He was dazed but not out.

"Trying to steal my car, asshole?"

"Please, n—no," he gurgled and wheezed with unfocused eyes.

"Please no? You're hilarious, dude."

"It wasn't...wasn't our idea. It was the scary bitch. It was her, she—"

CHAPTER TWENTY-FIVE

Julie "Trusty Lesbo" McCall stood behind the cargo box of an eighteen-wheel tractor-trailer and watched the tweakers she'd hired to ruin Kat's world fuck up royally. She wasn't totally surprised. How reliable could a drug addict really be? She had given them a nice chunk of rock and a .38. She had lifted the gun from one of the tent houses, so if there was a murder and it was traced back to the homeowner, what the hell did Trusty care? It was disruptive. She'd given the tweakers instructions to hurt either one of the hot martial artists or both—just make it look like a robbery gone bad, she'd told them.

When she saw them tumble out of the gym giggling like schoolgirls and waving money around, she knew they'd actually pulled the robbery off but hadn't harmed the girls. What she hadn't predicted was the hot Asian coming outside and kicking ass the way she had. *Total fucking turn-on.*

Trusty lost the grin on her face as she looked at that lucky bastard Crasher turning up and playing hero—again. *How in the fuck...*

She couldn't hear every word that was said, but she caught enough to know that the scrawny fucking tweaker had just given Crasher a detailed description of her and the whole story. Once Crasher had gotten all he needed Kat stepped to the tall fuck and slammed him in the temple with her elbow.

Gorgeous technique...

The dude's legs folded under him like an accordion. Some fat kid kicked him in the gut for good measure. Trusty used the semi-truck to block her exit from view. She moved to the fence behind her, scaled it and climbed into her car. Sirens inbound hit her ears as she drove out the back exit of the abandoned business. She decided one thing: No more games with the wannabe local news hero. Crasher had to go.

CHAPTER TWENTY-SIX

Before the cops showed up Kat gave me the rundown on the burglary attempt. The tall addict on the ground gave me a description of the woman who had hired them. It chilled me out and brought me right back to the taser woman in the hoodie with the empty shark eyes. Kat gave me a quick introduction to her student Alfred.

"Alfred, Lou Crasher. I gotta say, nice job with the nunchuks. Dangerous but nice."

His face flushed, "Thanks."

"Thank you. You really helped us out here. You're one brave cat."

"Cat?"

"Dude."

"Oh yeah, cat is like old-timey, right?"

"Old ti—? No. It's hip, nostalgic and cool, like classic rock. Do you like classic rock, buddy?"

He said it was okay for old-timey music. Kat sent him back inside as the cops rolled up. Kat and I exchanged a quick hug as the black-and-white pulled to a stop. Cops took statements and loaded tweakers into rides. Parents were called and were on the way to pick up kids. Kat was going to wait with the kids then call me later. She wanted all the details on the mysterious woman who had hired drug addicts to go after her and her students. She was pissed with me but tried to hide it.

I felt like absolute crap bringing my mess into her life and little more than freaked out that children could have been hurt. I needed to find this hacker and get her off the chessboard but soon. Before I cranked the engine over, I texted Jake a pic of the hacker's tattoo image with a note asking: *Disruptor. Can you look into this?*

Meredith Billups called as I crawled south on the 101 Freeway. She sounded drained—a woman beaten.

"Anything new, Lou, anything at all? I need to know what happened to my baby."

"There's a hacker, a woman. She's been turning up. The more I groove down this rabbit hole the more havoc she wreaks."

"I'm so sick o' these white bitches."

There it was again.

"I didn't mention her race, Ms. Billups."

Silence.

"You seem fixated on the point. What aren't you telling me?"

"What? Nuthin'. I just want answers and I wonder if you the man who can get 'em."

She was trying to throw me off with an insult. She'd have to cut deeper than that.

"It's almost like you seem to *know* the tent gang and this hacker are white. Give it up, Meredith, if you want my help."

"Goddammit, you're a pest. I don't know nuthin' 'cept my son was dating some white girl and I told him, I *told* him they be nuthin' but trouble, and where is he now, Mr. Crasher? You tell me what good it did my Cody, runnin' with—"

She began to sob. Then I remembered the girl in the social media pics with Cody. I'd been meaning to ask Meredith about her. Now here we were.

"Tell me about this girl."

"Nuthin' to tell. I ain't never met her cause she damn well wudn't welcome in this house, nuh-uh—hell, no."

There was more to this girl Cody dated. A thought hit me.

"Meredith, do you have numbers for those friends of his that I met? Tyrone and Chicken Little?"

CHAPTER TWENTY-SEVEN

I sat in my ride and was about to dial Chicken Little's number. He seemed like the second tier of the food chain and hopefully the one who would talk. Something twisted in my gut. I was more than a little worried about the *Disruptor*; in particular what Nima had said about the size of the group. They sounded like an army and not only that, an army cloaked in the shadows. Was I truly on their radar, or was I just a pet project of the hacker's? The back of my neck began to warm as it does. I attempted the breathing technique I'd seen in the yoga videos Jake had pushed on me, but it wasn't working. In fact, it only pissed me off: a grown man sitting in a classic 'stang, panting like a Golden-doodle after an hour of chasing a tennis ball.

I sent Jake another text describing my hacker friend. It was a long shot, but maybe his contacts knew her by reputation. My phone buzzed immediately. Not even Jake is that fast. I checked the screen. It wasn't him.

"Tracy, hey, what's up, girl?"

"Are you free tonight for some rock 'n' roll?"

The image of her body's curves, nooks and crannies flooded my mind.

"I couldn't think of anyone I'd rather do more," I said.

"Slow down, tiger, I'm talking about a jam session. The studio called with an opening. Everyone's available. I'd love to get rolling with your boy, Bobby."

"He's not my boy, not by a long shot. What time? I've got to work at seven."

"Shit, they've only got seven till nine."

"That blows. I gotta work."

"Can't you get someone to cover?"

"Not at the moment. I'm the new manager and I'm under the microscope right now."

"I get it," she said, sounding disappointed. "But we've got some smokin' gigs coming up and we really need to get Bob rolling."

"I know, but like I said, work—" I let it float.

"Fine, we'll run it down without you." She was pissed.

"Are you up for a late-night visitor?" I asked, putting basement-floor bass in my voice.

"Probably be beat after the rehearsal."

That was a lie. She had more energy than two Energizer bunnies on three Red Bulls. Was I being punished?

"Beat," I said as a statement not a question.

"Yes, beat. Look, I gotta go."

"Okay, I'll—"

I was talking to air. My cell signal bounced off a satellite right back to me with a resounding, "She's gone, pal." I shook it off and made the call to Cody's friend, Chicken Little.

"Hey, Chicken, this is Lou Crasher, I met you and Ty at Long Beach, Cody's memorial."

"I remember. Whatchew want?"

"I'm makin' progress on this thing and—"

"Get to the point, bruh, I got shit to do."

"Who's the white girl I saw with Cody on social? The one that drives Ms. Billups insane."

He paused a moment. I heard him say "muthafucka" slightly away from the speaker.

"Come on, Chicken, what's her deal? Why does Meredith hate her so much? Is it nobody's-good-enough-for-my-boy syndrome, or did Cody knock her up or something?"

"Door number two," he said. "Okay, so now you know. Cody knocked that bitch up," he paused. "Nah, I shouldn't say bitch, she cool an eh'thing, but it was just fucked, you know?"

"No, I don't know."

"She wudn't gettin' no abortion, so Cody had to step up—he that kinda nigga."

"Hence, selling Addie to support the kid," I said.

"Hence? What, you Charles fuckin' Dickens right now?"

I ignored that. "So selling the drug, working security, was all about raising the kid? Not just riding out the suspension."

"Mm-hmm."

"You're right, dude, Cody was a standup guy."

"Fuck yeah, he was," he said. "Anything else? I gotta go."

"What's the girl's name?"

"Lindsay Day, real white girl name."

"All right, cool. We're good but I might call you again."

"Leave a message, I rarely answer this bitch—surprised I did this time."

"If Cody's your boy, you'll answer my calls," I said, getting pissed. He clicked off.

As I was putting my phone onto the console, a text came in from Jake. I slid the shifter into park and read the message.

The hacker goes by the name of Trusty Lesbo. Real name unknown. Address unknown for now. Has a girlfriend down in Redondo Beach. Name is Magenta, stripper. Will text address in five. Anarchist group: Disruptor info to follow. For now: they're dangerous A.F. Watch your six—your friends, too.

The A.F. of the text was the millennial abbreviation for "as fuck." This was all I needed. The last phrase was like a kick to the gut, as it reminded me of Kat and the kids.

My shift at the Joint went by like the purple haze Jimi Hendrix once sang about. I barely remember it. I couldn't shake the thought of battling with a dangerous anti-establishment group. And some Trusty-frigging-hacker running free out there with her taser unsettled me to say the least. I let Chicken Little's info tumble around in my brain. Did Cody's becoming a father have anything to do with his death, or was it just as it seemed: wrong place, wrong time, resulting in death by handgun.

When I'm hired to play music for an artist, I want to know everything about the song. I want to know the arrangement, style, tempo, time signature, dynamics involved, all of it. I've been that way with many things in life, and now I recognized I'm doing the same thing on this Billups case. I'm going for all the answers and I'm going to lay them out for Meredith like sheet music with notes in the margins—no matter what I find, no matter which direction the Disruptor assholes come from.

CHAPTER TWENTY-EIGHT

I locked up, hopped on the 405 Freeway south and pointed my ride's front end toward Redondo Beach. By the time I passed Los Angeles International Airport crazy winds had kicked up. Garbage and palm fronds blew all over the six-lane freeway. If I were mayor, I'd double up on the number of garbage cans in the city and triple the fines on littering. It was like driving through a snowstorm during whiteout. Between dodging debris and avoiding other vehicles doing the same debris-dodge dance, it was like running a gauntlet. Although the ol' gal is over fifty years old, she handled the situation like a boss. Occasional gusts rocked her frame on the vintage suspension, but she pushed right back until I could right the situation.

I took the Rosecrans exit, rolled down the ramp heading west and merged onto Rosecrans. The wind kept up her protest, nearly knocking me into the car beside me as I hung a hard left on Aviation Boulevard. Every half-block or so my ride shook as if Godzilla had given her a hip check, but working together, we held our line. Moving through the intersection at Manhattan Beach Boulevard a gust shoved us into the oncoming traffic lane. I hauled the wheel back to the right, narrowly missing a black MINI Cooper. My eyes met the driver's briefly. We shared the same "holy shit" expression. The road wound down to the Pacific Coast Highway, taking me south through Hermosa Beach toward

Redondo. I'd have to have luck on my side in that the so-called Trusty Lesbo would be paying her gal a visit while I pulled my surveillance. If nothing else, I'd get the lay of the land and scope out decent vantage points for a return visit if it came to that. Trusty stepped into my life and now I'm treading through hers—in steel-toed combat boots.

I had no illusions about the stakeout game being as simple and profitable as it is in Hollywood movies, which is probably why I'll never let go of my day job.

The palm-frond count went up twenty-fold. I even turned on my wipers as if that would do anything. My ride shook and the windows rattled but I made it to Lucia Street intact and slid into a spot three houses from the address Jake had given me. I shut the ride down and listened to the howling wind; it was clear, the wind was pissed off about something. I got out and crossed the street. A blast of wind shoved me forward like a prison guard shoving me toward my cell. I posted up behind a lamppost and watched the cozy bungalow from afar. Tiny wind funnels spun food wrappers, newspapers and palm leaves in front of the home like it was a decorative art piece. The house lights were on in the front of the house, but I could see no bodies inside. A car approached from my left. I hauled out my phone and pretended to watch a video. I'm sure the driver was focused on driving through the mess, but caution is the way to go. As the car passed, I thought I saw two bodies move through the front room of the bungalow. I decided to take a look. Maybe the element of surprise would be enough. But what would I do once I got there? Surely Trusty would plunge into fight mode. Never one to shy away from a fight, I had to admit that battling it out with women is nowhere on my bucket list or any part of my DNA. Still, the hellion did tase my ass. As I marched to the door I clenched and unclenched my fists, cracked my neck and flexed my back muscles. My breathing rate increased. Even though the wind was cool and taking potshots at me, I steadied my legs and felt my ears heat up.

I told myself that by surprising her and warning her off while making it very clear I knew where to find her, she'd reconsider making me a project—but I didn't believe a word of it. It was about to be on.

I vaulted the steps, taking the final three in one bound and pounded hard on the door. I pounded non-stop, the only way to go—let's get it done. A burgundy-haired woman with a Pilates-sculpted body and thick, black eyeliner framing expressionless gray eyes flung the door open. She had a fake Marilyn Monroe beauty mark on her cheek.

"What?" she was forced to shout.

Her purple and black Japanese kimono fell open, revealing perfect C-cup breasts. She didn't fear the two-hundred-and-twelve-pound brother on her stoop in the slightest.

"I'm looking for your girlfriend, the Trusty-fucking-Lesbo."

"Fuck off," she said, stepping back and about to shut the door. The kimono opened, revealing a muscular thigh, no doubt from hanging upside down on a pole. Before the door closed, I got a clear view of her shotgun bungalow. A dog barked as it came toward the front door. Meanwhile, a darkly clad figure pulled a hoodie over its head and hustled toward the back door.

Trusty...

"Hey," I shouted, stepping forward, only to get the door slammed in my face. I pounded once then hopped down the steps. I hung a hard right down the narrow walkway between the bungalow and the neighbor's house. Moving fast, I had to avoid low-hanging jasmine from the neighbor's yard. At the end of the run a large electrical box nearly took half my face off. I emerged into a long narrow backyard. Debris flew everywhere, making the place look like a phony movie-set-of-a-disaster movie. Trusty was three-quarters of the way down the yard, heading toward a back fence. As I was about to take off after her, movement to my right caught my eye. A large brown Rhodesian Ridgeback barreled down the back wooden steps, coming at me with heat.

"Shit," I said, taking off in a sprint. A children's jungle gym loomed twenty strides in front and to the right of me. I hauled ass toward it but didn't make it. A sharp pain hit me just below the butt cheek. The Ridgeback fought to dig his fangs in deep, but I managed to spin away. A child's wagon was to my left. I grabbed it and got it between the dog and me. An annoying sting sprung from my right shoulder once, then a second time to the chest. I looked up through the haze of garbage and flying dirt to see Trusty's girlfriend standing half-naked in a marksman's pose, firing a pellet gun at me.

Wow, in high winds no less, she's good...

The Ridgeback leapt high toward me. I raised the wagon, put my size eleven throwback Adidas behind it and shoved wagon and K-9 backward. I spun on a dime and horsed it to a play-slide of the jungle gym and ran up it. The dog tried to follow but his claws slipped on the stainless steel. I reached a precarious rope and wood drawbridge and ran south along it. I took another pellet to the back. I heard her scream, but it was unintelligible. The dog paralleled me on the ground, barking and leaping at the drawbridge. At the far end of the bridge was a small three-by-three lookout platform. Beyond that, six or seven feet below and away, was a cedar-plank fence that Trusty had scrambled over. Formulating a plan on the run, I accelerated to the platform, timing it so my right foot landed square. I leapt up and out, pumping my arms and legs and praying for all kinds of for-giveness. I sailed over the snarling K-9 and began my descent. I was barely going to clear the fence. Or so I thought. My lead leg cleared the fence, but my back toe caught the top of the fence. This flipped me head over feet, slamming me hard into the fence on the neighbor's side where I involuntarily completed the full somersault and landed hard on my back in the neighboring yard.

The stars in the sky seemed to triple in number. I lay puffing on the ground, willing myself to get up. When I heard an incom-ing guttural growl, I had all the incentive I needed. Pushing up to a seated position, I saw a fast-moving Rottweiler coming in hot.

What's with all the dogs?

He had a wide barrel chest and must have weighed eighty-five pounds. No toy wagon would hold that hombre back. The dog came in from the house to my left. Directly in front of me was a pool that took up most of the yard. In fact, one side of the pool practically butted up against the neighboring cinderblock wall. Between the wall and the pool was a thin ledge no more than six inches wide—no way was this pool built to code, but what did I care? I hopped to my feet and flew to the pool and made it to the edge seconds before the big Rottweiler. With my back pancaked to the cinderblocks I shimmied at Mach speed along the ledge. I wasn't alone. Down near the deep end Trusty had had the same idea. She was nearly at the end of the pool near a fence that bookended the property.

"Enough of this shit, Trusty," I shouted through the howling wind and barking dog. She gave me a sinister grin from beneath the hood but said nothing. A teenage boy of about fourteen stood on the opposite side of the pool widthwise and repeatedly commanded his dog to attack.

"I'm the good guy, kid—the good—" But it was no use, the wind was too loud. Trusty made it to the property line, looked back at me with a smile, and climbed effortlessly over the wall. By this time the Rottweiler had plunged into the water from the shallow end and was swimming toward me. I shimmied faster and almost lost my footing. The teen was now filming me, great. The dog was a better swimmer than I was a shimmier. I stopped, hauled my wallet and phone out and tossed them over the wall Trusty had just scaled. As the big dog approached my feet, I dove over him into the deep end of the pool and swam toward the other side. I made it to the ledge and began to haul myself out when the kid stomped on my hand. Pain shot through my hand up my wrist. Initially I worried about my drumming career— until the Rottweiler's fangs sunk into my shoulder. With a grimace I pushed off the side, taking us toward the middle of the pool. Reaching back and around, I put my hand over the dog's snout, took a deep breath, plunged us just beneath the surface, and held us there.

The dog released the bite immediately. When we came up the dog was coughing and sputtering and heading for the shallow end. I made it back to the edge. This time when the teen went for the stomp, I reached up, grabbed his other leg and jerked it toward me, which sat him down hard on his tailbone.

"Look kid, you're doing the right thing here, but I'm the good guy. Ya see, in life—oh shit, here comes your dog. See ya, champ."

I boot it to the wall and clambered over without grace. I dropped to the other side and gathered up my phone and wallet. I took a knee and checked myself out. My shirt was ripped at the shoulder with a mild flow of blood escaping the dog-bite wound. I scanned the area for Trusty through the garbage storm. Up the block and across the street I spotted her hopping a chain-link fence into a plant nursery. With a curse I hauled my weary, two hundred and twelve pounds upright and took off at a good clip.

I'm not sure what Trusty's technique was with the barbed wire at the top of the fence, but I just powered through in the interest of time and cut myself all to hell. I crouched low and tried to listen, which was useless, so I watched instead. Where I landed had put me in a thickly packed field of dwarf blue palmetto palms, all in black pots. Many had tipped over or were falling, which fooled me several times into thinking the movement was my target. I kept low and continued scanning in all directions when I finally saw her. We were almost parallel twenty yards apart. I hit the deck and let her get ahead. Satisfied, I moved over and behind her and gradually closed the distance. Although she couldn't have heard me over the wind, something spooked her, causing her to suddenly spin around and bust me. In a quick movement she dove left. I pushed up and followed but quickly regretted it: she led us straight into the bougainvillea section. The thorns that tore at me were worse than the barbed wire. I was surely going to die of a thousand cuts—maybe two thousand.

"What's next, the cactus patch?" I shouted into the wind.

I quickly became disoriented. I wasn't panicked but I was pissed. Trusty was nowhere to be found. I emerged from the bougainvillea, then circled part of the perimeter, but I could feel in my bones that she wasn't hiding in the pretty but deadly area. I was about to admit defeat when, surprisingly, I heard rushing water. We were too far from the beach for it to be ocean. Without reason other than curiosity, I headed toward the flowing sound, which seemed to be coming from just over the rise of the muddy hill I was climbing. I had twenty yards to go when Trusty popped out of a stand of citrus trees. She didn't look my direction, just headed over the hill and disappeared from sight. I moved as quickly as the slick mud would allow, falling twice but instantly popping back up. When I crested the top, I saw a burst water main gushing hundreds of gallons of water onto the downslope I was now forced to navigate. I lost my footing and slammed down hard on my back. I recovered quickly and headed south with speed. A cardboard box slapped me in the face, but I pushed it aside and gained speed. I made out a figure at the bottom of the hill, and as I got closer, I could see it was Trusty; she was crouched in a low, athletic stance with a pitchfork in her hands.

Are you serious?

Now I was sliding, and I had nothing—no weapon and no control. I fought to get up but was only able to get a knee beneath me and use it as a rudder with my lead foot to steady my rapid descent. I held my hands up like a boxer and slid to my doom. Trusty shifted her weight slightly, making sure that when she gored me like a pig it would end me for good. I was within fifteen feet. She quickly pulled her hood back, revealing a close-cropped haircut. There may have been a head tattoo; I couldn't be sure. At the four-foot mark I hauled my back leg forward and flattened myself on my back. With speed nearing thirty miles an hour my legs perfectly torpedoed the pitchfork-wielder. She didn't make a sound as she sailed over my head. It had to hurt. I slid on for another twenty feet before coming to a stop. I jumped up, ready for action. Trusty was back up, heavily favoring her left leg. She bared her teeth and readied her attack when a spotlight hit her.

"Hold it, police!"

Two cops with guns over flashlights were coming in hot from my right. Trusty dropped the weapon and sprinted for the fence. She had thirty feet to go to an area where the fencing had a big hole in it—lucky break! I took off, tipping plant carts in my wake. I heard the cop who pursued me utter the f-word. He must have tripped or slipped. I didn't look back; never look back. I reached the front gate, which was locked with a loose chain. I got low and squeezed through. The flashlight caught my face. I barely heard the cop's order but ignored it. I crossed the street and ran between two houses, hopped the fence and jogged onto the street behind.

I was soaking wet, bruised and bleeding, but I wasn't going to be a guest at Redondo Beach P.D. Hotel if I could make it back to my ride. Three blocks later I slowed to a walk, pulled out my phone and got Jake's voicemail.

"Jake, it's Lou. I had the hacker but she got away. It ain't over but for now I feel like the drummer who showed up for the gig but forgot his drums."

CHAPTER TWENTY-NINE

Jake heard his phone vibrate from the other room where it sat on the large coffee table carved from British Columbia Sitka Spruce driftwood. The girl who nestled under his arm stirred with a moan. Jake looked down and saw a smile on her face as she breathed heavily. When she'd called she seemed upset and needed relief. Jake was happy to oblige; he had nothing going on. He lay on his back and stared at the ceiling. The woman's name was Heather, sweet girl. She claimed to work commercial real estate out of Phoenix and was hoping her company would transfer her back to L.A. It was all a lie, but Jake figured she was probably harmless. L.A. was a city of many more stories than angels. He didn't think he needed to research her. She had a good vibe about her, although sadness rested just beneath the surface. He trusted her, especially since she had come to his aid during the airplane altercation and then burst into the courtroom to vouch for him. That was stand-up—solid.

This was the third time they had hooked up. The first time was after the flight, which was only natural. Heather had stayed the night and most of the following day. They hit every sex position and on just about every weight-bearing surface in his warehouse loft. After the court case, which was tossed, the sexual encounter was gentler. She looked into his eyes more often and whispered sweet words as if she wanted a deeper connection with him.

Tonight was different still from the first two encounters. Never a dull moment, Jake thought. This time the sex had stress and desperation and, unfortunately, fear tied to it. It wasn't Jake she feared, it was someone or something else that had her on edge. Jake knew that maybe now was the time to do some research on Heather—she might need his help. While she slept after the first round, he got out his phone and reached out to his guy. Jake would know who she was and what she needed in forty-eight hours, less probably. He was about to get up, check the phone and grab water for them both when he felt her hand on his genitals.

"Where do you think you're going?" she asked with eyes closed.

Jake shifted so he could kiss her. She continued stroking during the lengthy kiss. When their lips parted, she eased a leg over and climbed on top.

"Oh, fuck yes," she said as he slid up inside her. Her head rocked back as she did a slow grind with her hips. Eventually her head came forward. With hands on his chest she smiled at him. Jake moved a hand to her ass and thrust deeper. She cried out and squeezed her eyes shut. She gasped and tensed up her body and held her spot. There it was. She seemed to come easier with each round. Jake wasn't done, he kept up the heat—he was going to give her another orgasm. And then he'd find a way to help her.

CHAPTER THIRTY

I walked with a slight limp at a half-mile an hour—faster than a toddler-aged escargot. I was soaked from pool water and painted in mud. Barbed wire and bougainvillea thorns had done their part in cutting me to shreds. The dog bite at my shoulder throbbed, same as the bite on my ass, but the good news was that I could hardly feel the puncture wounds from the pellet gun. The palm fronds and garbage kept up their whirling dance. I was too tired to dodge the smacking from all angles by fast food wrappers, newspapers and even one used diaper—thankfully the elastic held! Each time headlights approached I took to the shadows or slid behind thick trees. If a cop rolled along, I'd be up for a stop-and-frisk, no question. And if said cops were the guys from the nursery, it'd be all she wrote.

As I rounded the final corner a Starbucks cup hit me in the face. Why can't people finish their extra foam-whipped caffeinated bevies before they toss them? Shawn Kensington would call them shit-pricks and I'd have to agree. The vision of my Mustang parked at the curb a half-block ahead lifted my spirits tenfold. It was as if I'd fallen overboard off a booze cruise and finally caught sight of land. I unlocked her and climbed in. I removed the steering wheel club, put it in the locked position and set it on the passenger seat, ready in case Trusty leapt out of the windstorm. I cranked the engine but she sputtered and didn't take. I tried a second time. She coughed, gave it her best, then died.

"What is it, girl?"

My thoughts went to Trusty. Had she tampered with my gal? If so, we're talking grounds for murder. Then I remembered. My ride, being north of fifty years old, needs T.L.C. I went to the trunk and pulled out a five-gallon jerrycan of gas. I popped the hood and removed the carb cap. With a slightly trembling hand, I poured a small amount of gas into the carburetor. The carb mixes air and fuel but sometimes in older rides there's not enough fuel in the mix to ignite the start. While I was at it, I checked the oil; she was low. I grabbed a quart and a paper funnel from the trunk and topped it off. Classic car owners need semi-mechanic's garages in their trunks. It's the price of doing classic business. I put everything back in place, patted the dash and said, "Let's get it, baby doll." The ol' gal roared to life on the first try.

As I shifted into drive a loud thud came from my roof. I went into action without thought. Grabbing the steering wheel club, I jumped out and assumed a fighting stance. It turned out a large palm bough had fallen from the tree I was parked under. I pulled the branch off and climbed back into the car. Once my heartbeat returned to normal, I slid into drive and headed for the freeway. I contemplated a sandwich when I got home but decided against it—a three- to four-fingered Macallan over two rocks would better suit my ailments. *Had I remembered to chill a tumbler?*

The shower was a mixture of pleasure and pain. As blood and soapy water flowed down the drain, I took the time to roll the case around in my head. It felt like the more entangled I got with the hacker the further away I got from being of any use to Meredith and Jake. Maybe I'd met my match.

I toweled off, put on sweatpants and a Bob Marley T-shirt and poured myself a Macallan. I flipped on the TV but kept the sound off. A commercial with a group of young bikini-clad women was on. It took me until the end of the ad to figure out what they were selling. Turned out the amazing lifestyle where everything's a rooftop pool party was made possible by a cell phone provider.

The final shot focused on a skinny girl in a pink bikini with oversized sunglasses and lenses shaped like a bumble bee's eyes. The image rocked me. Where had I seen those shades before? Someone recently. I had it a second later. At least two people wore those shades. One was Cody's girl in one of the Facebook photos. I nearly kicked myself when I placed the second girl. It was the mourning coed at Cody's shrine on the Long Beach campus—the woman who had skittered off when I spoke to her. She'd been wearing a crocheted sweater with a hood and big bumble-bee glasses. Cody's girl, and I'd missed her.

Come on, Lou...

CHAPTER THIRTY-ONE

The next morning opened with a cool seventy-two degrees but experts claimed it would be in the nineties by early afternoon. The only color against the blue sky was five white wisps from airplane contrails. I hustled over to Meredith's. Every time I approached her door I felt ten pounds heavier. Constantly visiting a grieving mother was beyond my element. In the movies, cops visit once, the mother collapses in the doorway and in the next scene, the cops are back in the cruiser doing police jazz.

To my surprise Meredith seemed perky, which made my job a little easier, which, in turn, immediately made me feel selfish. What the hell did my level of comfort matter? I hadn't lost a son. I made the assumption that Ms. Billups's upbeat mood was due to a mother grown tired of weeping and attempting to pull it together.

"Come in, come in," she said, holding the door wide. "You say you might have something?"

"Maybe. May I see Cody's room? You can accompany me if you want."

Her face fell. "I'm not ready to go in there quite yet. You're welcome to it, just don't take nuthin'."

"Of course not," I said, moving past her.

Cody's room was almost spotless. He was well organized, just shy of OCD. His walls had posters of football players from an era long before his own. He had posters of Jim Brown, the 1985 Chicago Bears, and running back great Walter Payton. Sharing the wall real estate were rappers Tupac Shakur and Biggie Smalls. His five-drawer dresser needed a paint job but the clothes inside were folded with military precision. A laptop on his neatly organized desk was dead with no charger in sight. His bookshelf contained some heavy hitters: Langston Hughes, Steven Biko, Nelson Mandela, Toni Morrison, Maya Angelou, W.E.B. DuBois and more. A picture was coming together. Chicken Little appeared to be right: this Cody was a good kid. Nothing, except for a twelve-by-twelve-inch wooden box, lay under the bed. I pulled it out and took a look. Inside were mostly ticket stubs from lectures, readings and live music shows he had attended. Underneath the pile was a cell phone. I'd have thought the police would still have his phone, and they probably did. This was a different phone, a backup. I wondered if my positive image was about to be shattered. I tried powering it up, but it was dead. I was in luck, however, because a charger was in the glove compartment. I plugged it in and to my surprise it came to life. It was unlocked.

I went straight for the photos and found several pictures of Lindsay Day. There was a perfect shot of her sitting on the front steps of a small bungalow. Her straight black bangs were spirit-level straight across her forehead. She was smiling in that don't-take-my-picture sort of way. She seemed happy. I moved to the settings section of the phone and opened the "all photos" portion. The gods smiled on me. The smart phone's locator had been turned on for all of the photos. Many had been taken at the small home, which was not ten minutes from where I stood. There was a shot of her lying clothed but in a sexy pose on top of a comfort-er. The address was the same as the porch-step shot. It was also Lindsay Day's home.

I'm coming over, doll…

I slid the phone and charger into my pocket, put the box back under the bed, and then joined Meredith at her kitchen table.

"Get anything?"

"Maybe. I'm running something down that Chicken Little touched on."

Her eyes were expectant and bored at the same time. "Running something down don't tell me shit, Mr. Crasher. You don't think I can get whatever I want outta Chicken?"

"The girl, Lindsay Day, I'm going after her. I need to talk to her. That's all."

She waved a hand, "That bitch ain't got nuthin' we need, young man."

"We won't know until I talk to her. Gotta go. I'll keep you posted."

"You *better* keep me posted, shit."

CHAPTER THIRTY-TWO

I sat in my ride outside Lindsay Day's tiny bungalow. Two teens in rock T-shirts and baggy jeans rolled by on skateboards. They spoke loudly to each other because of the earbuds in their ears. A Native American woman who was fitness-instructor fit jogged by. She made the heads of all passing pedestrians turn—male and female. As she passed a neatly trimmed cluster of bird-of-paradise plants, a figure stood partially concealed and took in the sight. I did a doubletake as I recognized the man as Tyrone, Cody's friend. What the hell was he doing there? He had my full attention. Once the jogger was out of sight, he moved his eyes to Lindsay's home. We were staking out the same joint. I knew my business, what was his? He sucked on a vaporizer pen with one hand and pulled a portion of the birds of paradise back with the other to gain a better view.

A short East Indian woman came out of the house. Tyrone speed-walked down the street when he saw her. When she got to the sidewalk, she looked in his direction and held her gaze. The slow headshake told me she recognized Tyrone, which meant it wasn't the first time Tyrone had played peek-a-boo with Lindsay. A full ten seconds passed while she was deciding whether to call out to Tyrone. With a quick body shiver followed by throwing up her middle finger she briskly walked in the opposite direction and climbed into a white Smart Car with red trim. I guessed she was Lindsay's roommate. I took her departure as my cue and padded up the walk, hopped the three steps and put two knuckles to the door. A moment went by before the curtain beside the door was pulled back. Lindsay and I locked eyes. I smiled, not wanting to intimidate.

"Hello Lindsay, Lou Crasher. I was an acquaintance of Cody's."

"How come I don't know you?"

"I haven't seen him since I coached him in Pop Warner football. That's why I said acquaintance."

She held my eyes, considering. The curtain fell down and the door opened.

"Come on in," she said, standing back and looking at the floor. She closed the door as I stepped in. My eyes took in the small living room in a quick sweep.

"I'm so sorry for your loss, Lindsay."

"Thanks. What is it you want?" she asked, motioning me in. I sat on the edge of a plush lounger and interlaced my fingers with forearms on my thighs.

"I wasn't totally honest with you while I was on the other side of that door, but now that I'm here I won't bullshit you."

She folded her hands in her lap and held her lips in a tight straight line.

"I am Lou Crasher, that part was true. I did play and coach football but not Pop Warner with your boyfriend. I'm trying to catch the tent gang and Cody's killer, which may in fact, be the tent gang."

"You don't look like a cop, are you a private dick?"

"I look into things, yes."

"So, no license."

"No license, but I get results."

That seemed to satisfy her.

"I know about the baby, the Adderall, Cody's suspension, all of it." Why beat around the bush?

She put her head down and put her face into her hands and wept. A mini box of Kleenex sat on the glass-top coffee table.

She'd obviously been at the tears awhile. I slid the box toward her. She grabbed a handful and blew her nose.

"Fuck," she said. I gave her a moment, then told her how sorry I was.

"You said that already," she sniffled.

"I know. I met Chicken and Tyrone. You know they speak pretty highly of you, they respect you." She shrugged her shoulders.

Without looking my way, she let it all out. "I didn't want to keep the baby, you know, in the beginning. It was Cody. She's a gift, he said. Eventually I came around to like the idea, you know?" She looked up at me briefly then back at the floor.

"We knew it was going to be a struggle, but it was going to be worth it, even if his mother hated me. And it's not just because she's racist, she just fucking hates me!"

She grabbed more tissues and blew her nose. "And then, then...that fucking job. That fucking...security, fuck! I mean what kind of burglars take guns to rob an empty house? It's bullshit."

It was a good point, and I agreed with her. As I took in more of her place, I stopped on her body and studied her. I could have been looking at actress Jessica Alba's younger sister but with darker hair and straight bangs. She had on a blue Trump T-shirt where the president's face was the ass of a donkey. Her toned arms were cappuccino with milk brown. Both knees of her nicely fitted jeans were torn and apparently by the manufacturer prior to being shipped from the warehouse. Her bare feet had burgundy-painted toenails. Thick lashes accentuated her calico-cat yellow eyes. Through all that beauty I noticed one thing missing—a baby bump.

"Do you mind me asking how far along you are, Lindsay?"

The tears came hard and her body shook. Through heavy gasps she said, "Cody died. And when he died I felt something, something awful...an awful change, like fucking immediately."

Oh shit...

"You...lost it," I said quietly. Her whole body quivered. I got up and put an arm around her. She allowed it and sobbed into my chest. "I miss him so much!" she was saying for the third time when the front door opened and the woman I'd seen leave earlier entered.

"That fucking Tyrone was lurking again, fucking stalk—Oh, Linds, sweetie," she said, dumping her pharmacy bag and rushing to her friend's side. I got up and moved away. She hugged Lindsay and asked, "Who are you? What did you say to her?"

Lindsay told her it was okay and that I was helping catch the tent gang. Her roommate mellowed a little but continued to put the suspicious eye on me as she consoled her friend. Lindsay managed to pull it together. Her roommate made us strong coffee. The jolt was nice. We fumbled with some small talk before Lindsay interrupted her roommate and said, "You know, it seems weird, but I can't help but think that Meredith knows something about Cody's—his death. I know that sounds fucked, especially since she and I were—I don't know, it's just a feeling. Although if anything I thought she'd try something with me. That bitch terrifies me, for whatever it's worth," she trailed off.

Lindsay's roommate Sandra continued to console her friend while we drank our coffee. When I was finished, I moved us back to business.

"Tyrone. Outside. Why?"

Both ladies' eyes darted for the other, then parted ways as if nothing had happened. It was the worst playact I'd ever witnessed.

"Ladies, I'm the first to admit I'm a sucker for a pretty face, and right I now I've got two of 'em in front of me. That being said, I ain't as dumb as I look or sound," I warned. "So give it up. What's Tyrone's story?"

Lindsay worked at a hangnail on her thumb while Sandra studied the label of one of the vitamin bottles she'd brought home earlier.

"Really? Nothing? So I'm the only one who wants to find Cody's killer?"

"No," Lindsay mumbled.

"Look, I'm going to get to the truth of this thing sooner or later, so if it turns out you had info that would have helped me but that you withheld, well—I don't know, maybe the cops might look at it as obstruction," I said, reaching for legal straws. "And if they squeeze me for info on you, I'd have to come clean," I said, reaching further still.

"He's just concerned for Linds is all," Sandra lied.

"Which is why you weren't pissed at all about him stalking your door," I said, laying on the sarcasm.

"Don't be so smug, dude," Sandra said.

"Then don't bullshit me," I said, rising from my counter stool and pacing behind the ladies, which was meant to cause unease.

The girls remained locked up tighter than my drum-hardware case until finally, Sandra let loose a heavy sigh. "I think you should go, Mr. Crasher, Lindsay's tired.

"Is Lindsay tired?" I asked her directly. She nodded her head slowly. It was all I was going to get today. However, they gave me more than they had intended because sometimes when a dame locks up it speaks volumes. I scooped up Lindsay's phone, which I noticed was unlocked.

"Hey, what the fuck?" She came at me, but I turned my back to her and expanded it as I entered my info into her contacts. I turned and handed her the phone. She snatched it from me and called me a jerk.

"If you decide to do the right thing, you know, for Cody, I'm under C for Crasher."

My blood was up as I walked to the door and out to my ride. I scanned the area for Tyrone and decided that even as big as he was, if he were anywhere in sight I'd walk up to him and deliver a right fist to the button. I knew why I was pissed. The girls' stonewalling me put them on my suspect list. Why wouldn't the almost-baby-mamma help out the P.I. who's trying help her man rest in peace? Were she and her henchwoman Sandra involved in his death? It didn't feel right but one thing I know about people is they can be screwy. Maybe she lied about losing the baby and aborted it. Maybe Meredith was justified in her dislike of Lindsay. Maybe Cody had been a fling to Lindsay and getting knocked up queered things for the real lovers: Lindsay and Sandra.

I needed a beer and a sandwich. No, I needed to sit behind my kit and work out my frustrations. No, better yet, I needed Tracy to call me up and beg my forgiveness—a roll with her would smooth everything out. Hell, I even considered swinging by the Sick Tattoo Parlor and swill chilled bourbon with the beautiful Nima. Maybe she'd close early and one thing could lead to another.

I cranked up the ol' girl and was already feeling better listening to her purr. I let her idle as I planned my next move. A text came through. I didn't recognize the number.

Tyrone works at Pete's Scrap & Metal. Google it. Lindsay.

I was suddenly a man hatching a plan.

CHAPTER THIRTY-THREE

I found the scrap metal yard on Yelp and called and asked for Tyrone. I was told his shift started in an hour, which was exactly the length of time the Map app said it would take me to get there. No wonder he had skinned out from Lindsay's and hadn't returned. I shoved the floor shifter in gear and made tracks.

Visibility was next to useless. There was no way to get the ol' gal close enough for a good vantage point. The only option would be to go with a disguise. The problem with that is disguises only worked in 1970s television and updated Mission Impossible movies starring little Tom Cruise. As I pondered the situation, an elderly homeless woman pushed a shopping cart with two bad wheels past the scrap yard. Nobody paid her any attention—nobody.

Game on...

I fired up the ol' gal, pulled a U-turn and motored her to Ginny's Thrift Store. The only reason I knew about Ginny's was because I'd passed it on the way over and thought the inflated bear that was intended to lure shoppers inside was more corny than Kellogg's Corn Flakes. Yet, there I was, heading back there—ah, the power of advertising.

"Can I help you find anything specific?"

"I'll take two cans of whatever energy sauce you're on, baby. You're more perky than a game show contestant who's won a new car," I said.

The plump redhead jumped up and down on the spot and clapped her hands rapidly in front of her heavy jiggling jowls.

"I'm sorry," she squeaked. "I know I'm annoying, but I just love life, you know what I mean?"

I picked up a hint of Southern accent.

"Nothing annoying about loving life, young lady, I love Scotch much the same way."

She wagged a finger at me. "Oh, you rascal, you be sure and not love it too much now, ya hear. Because that could lead to problems." She tacked another laugh onto the end of her sentence. The glasses on the end of the silver daisy chain bounced up and down on her heavy breast like a dingy on rough seas.

"You're a ray of sunlight, Eunice," I said, clocking her nametag.

"Oh, bless your heart."

"I'm off to the men's section. I need a big overcoat...and such."

"Straight down that isle, and make a right at the end, hon'."

"Thanks, doll."

I left her fluttering and made my way to the coats. I found a standard gray raincoat that was one size too small for me and grabbed it. I pulled a beige pair of worn dress slacks two inches too big in the waist and a tacky brown long-sleeve pullover. For footwear I snagged a tattered old pair of Buster Brown dress shoes. The final accessories were a brown thin-brimmed porkpie hat, cheap white sunglasses, and a blue and white striped necktie I'd use for a belt.

"Boo," Eunice laughed. "Finding everything, sir?"

"Yes ma'am, I believe I'm done."

"Follow me and I'll ring you up, cutie pe-tootie."

"Eunice, you have a brother blushing out here."

He body rolls shook with laughter. A male voice came over the sound system and told Eunice to stop flirting with the customers. It ended with a "damn it!" that was slightly off microphone.

"Oh, just ignore that, sir, that's my husband. He's the jealous type."

"He'd have to be; look at you," I said.

She leaned in close and lowered her voice, "It actually makes things real hot in the bedroom," she giggled. "Oh, just shut me up, what's wrong with me?"

When I got to the counter, Eunice moved around to the cash register and stood beside a gent who seemed asleep on his feet.

"Okay, let's ring ya up, handsome."

"Eunice, dial it down, would ya," the man said.

"The lucky husband?" I asked.

"What is says on the marriage license," he sighed.

"Oh stop, you grouchy bear," Eunice said, entering my items with a giant smile.

The husband over rolled his eyes as his wife told me for the fourteenth time to come back any time. Eunice walked me out, or more like ushered. When the door behind me closed she flipped the "Closed" sign around on the window. Nothing like an after-noon delight—glad I was able to be of help.

Back in the ol' gal I pulled my bowie knife from my glove compartment and cut random holes into the clothes. I bought three tacos from Chico's Taco truck. I ate one and used the other two to smear over the clothes and to this I added the extra sauce packets I had lifted from the truck. With the clothes all messed up, I found a gravel lot and mushed the clothes all around until the dust and sauce blended in a nasty mix.

Fifteen minutes later I was back at the scrap yard with dirt ground into my hands, under fingernails and smudged into my face. I didn't have the street body odor but figured it was okay since I wasn't planning on getting close to anyone. I parked at my former spot and shut down the ol' gal. I vacillated about whether to take my steering wheel club with me. Feeling paranoid, I found myself sliding it inside the undersized overcoat. I affected a limp and loped toward the salvage yard's chain-link fence. Keeping my head down as I moved, I scanned left and right and was satisfied that, sadly, like most homeless folk, I was invisible. I stumbled and fell onto the fence and leaned against it as if I were too tired or drunk to get up.

Business carried on as expected at the yard. Cars came in on flatbeds for donation or salvage, and half as many people showed up looking to buy parts for their rides. I almost became distracted by some of the classics being hauled in and made a note to come back and shop for parts at the business. Luck was on my side as Tyrone, along with a handful of other guys, worked in the yard just feet from my resting spot. Dialog was easily heard. Unfortunately, most of it was from the blue-collar workingman's playbook: A lot of "muthafuckas," "bitches," homophobic slurs, and laughter. One thing I couldn't deny was that although I'm sure the job was low-paying, these guys seemed to have a good time. I wondered if my plan was a bust. What the hell of use was I expecting to hear at this place? And how long would I have to sit on the hard sidewalk playing down-on-my-luck?

After an hour I noticed some vehicles pull in and turn around fairly quickly—too quickly for shopping. I craned my neck around for a better look. Five minutes later a calf cramp kicked in, so I decided to lay flat on my side like I'd passed out. I began to notice a pattern. The quick-stop rides would pull into the lot and head toward a trailer with faded paint and several rust spots. Tyrone would approach and lean his head in the window. The chat was always brief, then he'd trot over behind the trailer and return moments later. An exchange would occur, and the customer would be on his, or sometimes her, merry way. Drug deal. I've been in the music business too long not to recognize it. I dug out my phone and took a few pics. I took mental inventory on Tyrone's previous five customers, their rides in particular: a brunette in a Volkswagen Cabrio; a surfer dude in a BMW 3 Series; a bottle blond in a brand new Tesla—the baby version; two stoners in a Land Rover—the sporty "Evoque" version; and a gender-fluid type cat in an Audi S4. All users probably were between eighteen and twenty-two. I'd seen rows of these vehicles and ones like them on the Long Beach campus lot. Tyrone was selling to college students, and I'd bet sugar cookies to snare drums that the cat was selling Adderall.

That sucka done took over Cody's business...huh.

"Hey," a raspy high-pitched voice said before kicking me in the back near the kidneys. It scared the crap out of me more than it hurt. I hadn't heard him approach. I rolled over and got to my knees. A stocky looking gent in a Pete's Scrap & Metal shirt frowned at me.

"Get the fuck outta here, loser, you're bad for business. I can't have you—"

"Are you hir—hiring?" I asked, slurring my words.

"Not you I ain't, now fuck off."

He came in as if to kick me again as I got to my feet. I cowered in fear.

"Okay, okay, I'm go—going," I whined.

"Hurry up, before I shove my Timberland up your ass," he growled. I turned to go.

"Will you do me one favor fir—first?"

"What? No. Fuck off," he said coming in fast. I fake cowered a split second then slid the club into my grip and came up hard from down low and caught him square in the nuts. He crumpled, making a bird chirping sound. Someone on the other side of the fence shouted, "Oh snap, the boss is down! That homeless nigga done fucked him up, boi!"

I got close to his ear. "The homeless are people too, asshole."

I flipped the club vertically and brought the butt end down hard on his temple. He went out. I popped up and sprinted off, running without the limp, and took a circuitous route back to the ol' gal. I leaned my ass on the trunk, panting hard, with my hands on my knees. I looked down at my steering wheel club and grinned. "Nice job, baby doll. I think I'm gonna call you Eunice."

I opened the passenger side of the car and got changed, half in, half out, back into my regular clothes. I got a few passing glances but no protests, seeing as most people prefer to mind their own business rather than getting involved. It felt good to be in my regular clothes but not as good as a shower was going to feel. It appeared Tyrone had taken over Cody's pill business. Would he have killed him for it? Maybe, he was bad-tempered enough—for sure. And people have killed for less, but how lucrative is selling Addie to college brats? One of the things I'd have to find out while I watched Cody's so-called buddy.

CHAPTER THIRTY-FOUR

A quick update call to Meredith was relatively painless. Naturally, I left out the Tyrone business. I wasn't sure how tight the two of them actually were. At work every band showed up on time and paid in full. Big Eddie Carruthers called in and gave me a verbal pat on the back for a job going smoothly, then mentioned a security company was coming by to install some cameras. My day was moving along like an 80s' rock ballad—cheesy, but you secretly like it and sing along when no one is watching.

The wrinkle in the day happened when the security company missed their arrival window by three hours. There was no love lost between the installer and me.

"You're kinda late, pal," I said.

"Yeah, we got hung up on—"

"Another job," I finished for him. "You guys, the cable guys, phone company—it's always the same old, 'another-job-ran-late' line."

He put his drill into his tool belt and took a step toward me. "What happened to your face? You been fighting? Cause if so, you don't look like you're that good at it."

"Oh no, I'm great, actually. I kicked the shit out of three security camera installers—drunk, no less."

"What's your problem...brother?"

"I gotta rehearsal to get to and you cats show three hours

late."

"You wanna reschedule? We can easily fuck off, but it'll be a week before we fit your ass back in."

He had a point. I'm not sure why I came at the guy so hard: probably because I hate being late for rehearsal.

"Point taken, champ. I apologize for being a dick. Carry on."

He hmphed me, then moved to the hallway to install the first camera. His assistant picked up a toolbox and whispered, "Sorry we're late, bro."

"No sweat."

If I thought that was the only hiccup of the day I was mistaken. The security team finally finished. After paying them and locking up, I pulled up to the rehearsal studio fifteen minutes late, which was twenty for me. I hauled my cymbal bag, snare drum, stick bag and double bass drum pedal from the trunk and headed toward the studio but stopped in my tracks.

Bob was in his car. He didn't see me coming. He was hunched over his console about to do a line of cocaine. I dropped my gear, which is something I never do, and pounded on the roof of his car. He spilled the line. White powder went all over the interior and his face.

"Get the fuck outta there, Bob! What the fuck!"

He hopped out like he was about to do something.

"Fuck you, Lou, this shit ain't cheap, man."

"Fuck me? Fuck you, Bob, you nearly kicked last time. I can't believe you're—"

"Mind yo business Lou. I ain't your bitch."

I stepped in fast, grabbed him by the collar and shoved him against his ride.

"Do I need to remind you of the coma, you dipshit?"

"Stay in yo lane, nigga."

"Nig—what the fuck you call me? I grabbed his throat with one hand and slapped him hard with my other."

"Hey! What the fuck, Crasher?" It was Tracy. "Let go of him, Lou. Jesus!"

I slapped him again—now that we had an audience. Bob over-sold the hit, staggered and fell to the ground.

"Get up, Bob, ya bullshitter."

"My God," Tracy said, helping Bob to his feet. "What's wrong with you?"

"He's doing blow out here."

"Ah, newsflash—he's a musician."

"He almost died last time, Tracy."

"That shit was spiked, Lou. This shit is good," Bob said.

I tried to get at him, but Tracy cut me off.

"Back off, Lou, I mean it."

"You're a fucking idiot, Bob," I said, picking up my gear. The rest of the band came out and watched the show along with a few band members from other bands.

"You know what, Lou, just take your shit and go home."

"Home? We've got to rehearse."

"We do, you don't."

The band members all wore similar sheepish expressions. I'd seen this film before.

"You sayin' I'm out?"

"Come on Lou, you blow off rehearsals, now you're twenty minutes late—I mean Bob's been working his ass off and you've been AWOL."

"AWOL?"

"Not to mention beating the shit outta my bass player."

"Those were wakeup slaps, I barely touched him."

A few members of another band laughed as they passed a joint around.

"Look, Lou," Tracy said, coming in close and softening her voice. "Just sit this next gig out. I've already got another gun-for-hire ready to go."

"I was the gun-for-hire that turned this gig permanent. Re-member?"

"It doesn't seem like you want it. But fuck it, it's just this next gig because—"

"So, is this like rock 'n' roll probation? Keep the hired gun, Cupcake. I'm out." I grabbed my stuff and put it back in the trunk.

"So, you're quitting then?" Tracy asked hands on her hips.

"That's what 'out' means, doll."

One of the laughing band members of the other band shouted, "Hey we need a drummer, but we don't want any wakeup slaps though, bro."

My ears were hot. The back of my neck was warm. I looked at the Tarts a final time. Bob spoke in a low voice, "Thanks for the gig, Lou. You're outta control, but thanks. Seriously."

I glanced into my ride and eyed Eunice, my steering wheel club. I shoved a violent vision to the back of my brain.

Move on, Lou...

I hopped in my ride, cranked her over and dropped hammer. The ol' gal kicked her back end out in solidarity.

Screw these lightweight musicians. I had a case to solve.

CHAPTER THIRTY-FIVE

Jake's grip was still solid on the loose ropes that were fastened to the overhead beam as he performed his thirty-fifth slow pull-up: five seconds up, hold for three, then down for a slow five-second descent. Once back on the ground he lowered all the way to the mat and held the splits for a minute on each side; right leg out in front first, then switched. After some gentle yoga poses, he walked on his hands to the open kitchen, slowly lowered his feet to the floor, and grabbed a water jug. A half-gallon gone, he glanced at his phone. His contact had sent a text. Jake skimmed it, then made a call.

"Hey," Jake said.

"Yeah."

"Is this accurate?"

"Ninety percent. Tomorrow night they hit the tenth house somewhere in the South Bay, beach cities. It may be a while before we get an exact—"

"No need, I gotta a guy," Jake said.

"Thought you might. So, you called about the other thing."

"You sure it's her?"

The man's silence was answer enough.

"Okay. I'll deal with that. What about El Paso?"

"Details in five."

"Copy that," Jake said.

Jake killed the call, then texted Lou what he knew about the tenth house. Lou responded immediately that he was going to sit on Moscow Mule. Jake's jaw clenched and unclenched. He moved toward the shower, stopped at his speed bag and unleashed a left-leg tornado kick, connected and followed with an immediate right spinning-heel kick. The bag bounced back and forth several times and continued rattling as Jake entered the bathroom.

CHAPTER THIRTY-SIX

I didn't know where I stood, other than barely three feet down a five-mile path to figuring out who killed Cody. Maybe I wanted it too badly because Jake had asked for my help and I wanted to impress him. If we live to impress, we live the life of a damn fool, my Uncle Curtis used to say, or words to that effect. It felt as if the answer were right in front of me but I was too busy trying to manufacture the killer: Against my better judgment, I was beginning to think Tyrone was responsible for Cody's murder.

The mess with Yesterday's Pop Tart was small potatoes compared with a murder case, but I was pissed. It seemed over before it began, especially the good times with Tracy. Women come and go, my uncle said, in all shapes, sizes, colors and creeds. Did anyone talk about creeds anymore?

I sat in my underground parking lot and pondered my next move. Only I didn't know what it was, which is why I was sitting in the ol' gal, running most of this down out loud—she'd always been a good listener. A text came in from Jake. The tent gang were going for house number ten in the South Bay. I'd be in motion—back to Moscow Mule's—then pull the tail. But what to do until then? My phone buzzed, giving me my answer.

Meredith wanted me to stop by. Odd, seeing as I'd already updated her. But a client is a client. The ol' gal boomed up on the first try. I launched out of the garage once the ages-old gate slid open.

I was about to put knuckles to Meredith's door when it opened. On the other side of the threshold to my limited surprise was Tyrone.

"We need to talk," he said.

I didn't say a word or move a muscle until he stood aside so I could enter. Meredith was at her usual spot, nursing a cinnamon chai.

"Before you niggas get started, you need to know I won't stand for any bullshit up in my house, ya hear?"

"Yes ma'am," Tyrone said.

"Why should there be any B.S.? I'm just trying to find Cody's killer."

"Cause you be pullin' shit at my work, nigga, that's why," Tyrone said, stepping close to me.

"You're bigger and younger but I promise you, you will get hurt," I said. It was enough to cause him to take a step back.

"That's better," I said. "Yeah, that was me. Me doing my job. I'm running everything down until the sands of confusion drift away and only the answers are left."

"Speak plain, nigga."

"You got more than sweet-ride owners lookin' for hubcaps 'n' carburetors out there, Tyrone—Ms. Billups know what you're slingin'?" I asked.

"I know what he be doin', Mr. Crasher. I didn't at first, but I do now," Meredith said.

"And you're okay with this man taking over your son's pill business?"

"Watch your mouth, ni—"

"And you have no problem with this cat hovering outside your son's ex-girlfriend's crib like a dog staring at a T-bone?"

"Why should I care? I was pissed my boy was sellin' and I damn sure don't give a damn about no white bitch trynna trap my boy, neither."

"You need to bounce, boy; me 'n Ms. Billups be family, we can handle this."

I put a hand to my forehead. My blood was at simmer level.

"Your son dies, and this fool takes over his drug business and goes after his girl twenty minutes later and you're cool with—are you kidding me, Meredith?"

Tyrone lost it, "Nigga, I done told you," he said, and charged me. I had more trust in the promise we had made to Ms. Billups about not busting up the place. Dumb play on my part, I thought, as I was tackled over the coffee table and slammed into the hutch. The large oak cabinet came down hard on me. Glass and picture frames scattered everywhere. I bench-pressed the cabinet off and crawled out feeling more than a little dizzy. I struggled to my feet. Tyrone was on me like a cyclone.

He was strong, but not a great fighter. He got some good shots into my mid-section but gained little effect. He went for a right cross to my face. I blocked it with a left and grabbed his throat with my right, hooked his ankle with my right foot and put him down hard, shattering Meredith's glass coffee table. I got two big haymakers into his nose and eye socket when I heard the shotgun rack and felt the end of the barrel on the back of my skull.

"I done told you niggas, no bullshit in my house," Meredith said calmly.

Tyrone spat blood out of his mouth and struggled to his side. I was already up and backing away from the Mossberg in Meredith's grip. Her pupils were coal black and set deep in a nasty squint. Her look said she'd fired a gun before, but I wondered if it said she'd killed before. It sure looked like it. I raised my hands and held her look while keeping Tyrone in my peripheral. He seemed upset I'd gotten the better of him. It happens all the time when guys who are accustomed to being king on the field get bested on the street. He rubbed his throat and grimaced and spat.

Without taking eyes or her gun off me Meredith spoke over her shoulder, "Spit again in my house T, and I'm turning this gun on you. You know better 'n that."

"Sorry, Ms. Billups."

Tyrone and I glared at each other over our cinnamon chai coffee cups. We were like two cage fighters sitting on stools between rounds. Bodies wound tight, ready for the bell, while struggling to appear relaxed. Every now and then he'd complain about his throat. I smiled on the inside, knowing I'd tuned up a bigger guy. It's not the size of the dog...

"Meredith, your text said you wanted to see me; well, I'm here. What have you got?"

"I called you here to tell you to back off Tyrone. You be barking up the wrong tree."

"The short answer is no. I don't work that way."

"You work for me, mutha—"

"I work for Jake. Can't be moved on that. And, in doing so, I find out Tyrone is going after everything Cody had five minutes after he's in the ground."

"Show some respect to his moms, yo. You up in her house," Tyrone said.

"When I'm summoned, and some idiot waits to jump me, I shove respect to the side. This was child's play. I hope you've got better moves on the field—junior."

Tyrone's jaw clenched and his breathing ticked up. Meredith tapped a ring finger on the barrel of the Mossberg that sat on her lap. Tyrone fell back in line. I got up.

"Text me later when you're ready to talk about why you really called me here," I said to Meredith, ignoring Tyrone. Half-way down the hall she called after me.

"You gon' pay for this mess!"

I came back down the hall and stood over Meredith. She gripped the Mossberg tight.

"Tyrone is going to pay for every damn thing in here with his Addie money," I said. "Or should I say, your *son's* money?"

Meredith leveled the gun at me. Tyrone flinched.

"I'm trying to find your son's killer while Tyrone, here, is trying to *be* your son, and the barrel's on me? The word curious comes to mind."

I walked out half expecting a bullet in the back.

CHAPTER THIRTY-SEVEN

Once again, the tent gang sat around Moscow Mule's guesthouse. They each had a glass of rose in front of them—the only one they'd have until the job was done. Moscow raised her wine glass.

"Ladies, we've had a good run and tonight we'll knock down number ten. I cased this place and it's a doozy. I think you'll be happy with the take."

They clinked glasses. "I heard that," I.P.A. said.

"But with that kid getting killed and the public putting pressure on the cops, we need to change course after this."

"Oh, thank God," Boilermaker exhaled.

"We're not quitting, fuck that, bitches," I.P.A. said.

"I said change. Hear me out. I've been looking at Package Droppers."

"That company that's trying to take on Amazon, right?"

"The same. They've got this delivery option where the delivery driver can drop the package at the house when the homeowner isn't home, but not on the porch, actually inside the home. There's an app, like the ring system. The driver has a temporary code, drops the package, then backs out of the home."

"Yeah, we've heard, so what's the play?" Boilermaker asked.

"We tail one of these fools, follow him in, and rob the place."

"So what do we do, Moscow, tie him up while—"

"You got it, bitch."

"I kinda like it," Boilermaker grinned.

"I don't know," I.P.A. said.

Moscow stood up and paced. "It's the best way to keep our thing going and, more importantly, we won't need that psycho Trusty bitch."

A silence fell over the room. "I take it you like that prospect?" Moscow asked, to which her partners nodded their heads.

"I like it," Boilermaker said. "But how big is this company? We might be driving all over town looking for these Package Dropper idiots."

"I considered that, so I say we add good, old-fashioned, rush-the-damn-door home invasions, too. Either way, the Trusty fucking Lesbo is out."

Her partners raised glasses. "The Trusty bitch is done," I.P.A. said as the glasses clinked.

CHAPTER THIRTY-EIGHT

Julie McCall—aka Trusty Lesbo—sat in her stripper girlfriend Magenta's spare bedroom and grinned. The room was jammed with portable wardrobe racks packed with stripper costumes. Trusty liked the idea that in her profession Lisa teased men all night long then gave up the goods to her, another woman.

Trusty had just finished giving her gal a goodbye she'd not likely forget. She'd rocked her so hard her moaning gasps had turned to tears. Trusty kissed her forehead and left the room. She couldn't believe how emotional some women could be. But that wasn't the only reason a smile was on Trusty's face. She had listened to the gang through Moscow's Smart robotic vacuum—so simple. She'd even hijacked it so that it basically circled the room the tent gang met in, and no one was the wiser. The tent gang's plot to ditch her after the evening's heist amused Trusty. They were in for the rudest of awakenings.

Disruptor was the perfect home for Trusty. They fucked with people, which is essentially what Trusty had been doing since she took her first breath. Her parents had sent her to a half-dozen counselors and shrinks before she turned thirteen. What about being wild, living life the way she wanted, didn't they understand? No, she wasn't abused, neglected or bullied, she just...was. Call her evil, bi-polar, hyperactive, borderline, she couldn't give two shits; whatever floated the boat of their psychoanalytical bullshit minds, she always thought.

As her gal pal slept, or cried, or whatever, Trusty arranged lodging along the way to New Orleans, her destination. A member offered to put her up in El Paso, more or less halfway between L.A. and the great state of Louisiana. She'd relax for a day or two in El Paso, then go on to New Orleans where she'd chill out for a couple months. The member who'd offered her the room didn't know she was about to be on the run for murders she was about to commit, but she was sure he suspected it was something heavy—she'd made a bit of a name for herself with *Disruptor*. In fact, the idiot was probably a superfan of her work—loser. She'd been with the group for just under three years and got a kick out of them. She liked the randomness of the mission and that there was very little structure. But what really kept her in it was there were a lot of talented members, people who were good at what they did. Anger can be a hell of a thing when focused and coordinated.

The door to the spare room creaked open. "Not now," Trusty barked.

"I just wanted to see what you're doing."

"Fingering myself, now fuck off."

"'Scuse me? It's my fucking house, bi—"

"You see what I'm doing, and I'll have to hurt you," Trusty said, leaping to her feet so fast Magenta jumped back out of the room. Trusty sat back down and listened a little longer to her pathetic, soon-to-be-dead crew. Well, they weren't all going to die, just I.P.A. and Boilermaker. She'd leave Moscow to hold the bag. A quick little tase and wrap her up for the cops to find. With ten houses under her belt and the taunting they'd given this town, Moscow Mule would probably get ten to fifteen years—out in eight for good behavior. And depending on where Trusty was at that time, maybe she'd visit the ex-con. Of course, if they pinned the security-guard murder on her, then the bitch was looking at life.

Trusty checked her watch. There was still plenty of time to get in place. She was getting moist down below again. Time to make nice with her oversensitive hot commodity and take her around the park again.

"Babe? C'mere a minute."

Footsteps came from the hall. The door opened a crack and Trusty could see Magenta's long hair partially covering the one eye she looked through. Trusty flashed a coquettish smile.

"You can be such a bitch," Magenta said.

"But this bitch gets you off like no other. Am I wrong?"

Magenta put a finger to her bottom lip and shook her head no. What a child, Trusty thought.

"Get in here if you want some of this dessert," Trusty said, letting the blanket fall to the floor. With slow theatrics she slowly opened her legs. Magenta came in fast and got down on her knees.

Like a bee to my honey...

Trusty's head rocked back. With eyes closed as she said, "Remember to finish everything on your plate, bitch."

CHAPTER THIRTY-NINE

Jake made arrangements with his contact to have a private pilot fly him to El Paso. If things didn't pan out for Lou with the tent gang, Jake wanted to throw a wrench into Trusty's escape plan. Four hours ago he'd received Intel from his contact who hacked FBI files. Jake had learned what he could about the Mission Hills neighborhood on the flight over. Houses were primarily built in the 1950s to 1970s with the median price being around two hundred and twenty thousand. Families as well as blue-collar workers and even some executives lived in the neighborhood. Real estate websites claimed the schools were good and the streets safe.

Now Jake stood in the shadow of a honey mesquite tree on Penny Lane in Mission Hills, watching the home of Stephen Bore. He had picked up the tail earlier at a convenience store where Bore bought potato chips, beef jerky, six single-liter bottles of Coke, three tins of beef stew, and four bottles of cheap bubbly. All of this was done with a dumb-ass grin on his face. He was the one tasked with putting up Trusty, the infamous hacker, while she was on route to New Orleans. Bore's grin surely wasn't because he thought he'd get some. The name Trusty Lesbo should have made that plain. No, Bore was eager to be the chosen one to house the famous hacker. What a loser.

Jake followed him back to his home and waited for the right time...to ruin his life.

CHAPTER FORTY

Stephen Bore twirled a pen through his fingers in one hand and worked his keyboard with the other. The Trusty Lesbo would soon be in his home—his home! He was totally living the dream. Once word spread his ranking would go up. *Disruptor* would consider him trustworthy and send him more "assignments." This was awesome.

The temperature seemed to drop suddenly, and he felt a chill at the back of his neck. He swiveled around in his chair.

"Hello?"

Hearing nothing, he spun back to his three-monitor bank, which he called the cockpit. He pulled his tattered cardigan tighter around his shoulders. As his fingers returned to his the keyboard he saw shadow pass behind him on the monitor. Barely maintaining composure, he reached for the mouse in an attempt to delete all things related to *Disruptor,* as per the rules. Before he could do so, his two hundred and thirty-eight pounds were easily hauled up and out of his chair.

"What the fuck!"

He was hoisted high and slammed down hard on the floor. He thought his spine was cracked for sure. He saw stars and thought he'd pass out. He looked up and saw a man who was six feet tall and weighed at least two-twenty.

How the fuck...

"End of the line, Stephen Bore," the gravelly voice said.

"Please no, I have cash."

"Save it for legal fees," the sinewy black man said.

"Okay, wait. I know you think I'm just some loner hacker who—"

"Sounds about right."

"But I'm not alone," he wheezed. "Homer!" he screamed.

A side door slid open and a man filled the opening. He was forced to duck his head as he entered.

"Meet Homer. I'm mentoring him, but as you can see by his dimensions, he has other uses."

Homer moved into the light and flashed a yellow-toothed grin.

"You can still walk away, Homer," the confident black man said.

Stephen Bore laughed out loud. The muscled black man swiftly raised his knee and stomped Bore semi-conscious without taking his eyes off Homer. Homer stepped backward and locked the door he had entered through.

"Last chance," the black man said.

Homer grinned and pulled a seven-inch blade from the back of his waistband. This made Bore, now slightly more alert, smile. His mentee was going to kill this fucking intruder and Stephen had a ringside seat. The smaller combatant picked up Bore's chair and circled to his left. Homer moved in the same direction and stabbed forward. The blade got stuck in the chair legs briefly before Homer yanked it back. Homer switched his grip and circled in the opposite direction. The black man followed suit and feigned a strike to the head before swinging the chair low and catching Homer on the side of the knee. Without hesitation Homer took to his good knee as he raised his massive arm to fend off a chair blow to his head. Upon contact, the chair broke apart. Stephen Bore thought that must have hurt like hell, but his guy was still in the fight.

"Kick his ass, Homer. You got this," Bore pleaded more than cheered.

Homer followed the chair strike with a backward slice with the knife. The black brother stepped forward and blocked the blow at the wrist with his thick calf. He grabbed Homer's wrist and snapped it around his calf muscle. Homer screamed. The blade dropped to the floor. Stephen wanted to reach for it, but he knew he'd never make it.

The tough black man picked up the blade, sprawled over Homer and pinned him. The next thing Stephen heard were gurgling sounds coming from his mentee as the blade was plunged into his throat. Bore thought back to all of the wonderful nights he and Homer had spent together and wanted to cry but was too afraid for tears.

In a panic, he crawled up his desk. He had to get to the mouse. But he was too late. He felt a bolt of pain to his hamstring. He looked back to see the blade protruding from his leg. He screamed as he saw the intruder move toward him with a casual expression on his face. Stephen collapsed back to the floor. The black man turned off the computer and stepped back. Stephen howled and was about to beg for mercy when the big man paused to take a phone call.

A phone call, seriously?

CHAPTER FORTY-ONE

Everybody's issue is bigger than everybody else's. Tracy had a band to run and she was going to run it her way. She should have given me more slack on the leash, but she didn't see it that way. Sure, it was bullshit that I'm out when I'm the guy who brought her the bass player, but I wasn't really pissed. I wondered why until I gave my head a shake. I was playing three songs at the same time: private investigator on a big case, gigging rock drummer, and rehearsal-space manager—and the jobs were butting heads. Tracy may have done me a favor, and not just because I had no desire to play with Bobby Coldwater, my so-called buddy. He'd screw things up soon enough and that would be on Tracy—I had warned her about the guy.

Bobby's moving in on my band, playacting the hero and not standing up for me was no surprise. Bobby takes life one day at a time with a leech's enthusiasm. If you've got something, Bobby will take it from you and act like you owe him. I wasn't worried about finding another band but figured I ought to go back to being a gun for hire. A full band commitment was probably too much to dance with the other two gigs. As these thoughts tumbled around, I opened my fridge. There was a mango that was going to be rotten within ten minutes, so I hauled it out, unsure about the last time I'd eaten fruit. I sliced it up and decided beer wouldn't go with fruit, so I pulled a bottle of flat champagne from the fridge door. Waste not, want not—right? As I looked at the bubble-less bubbly I popped a couple slices of the mango into the flute and wondered if I was going soft. Jim Rockford would never drink such a thing.

I moved back to the case in hopes of drowning out the soundtrack of The Tarts in my head and fired up the cell phone I'd swiped from Cody's bedroom. I went at the pictures again, paying more attention to details, and one detail popped up more than once. In at least three pictures of Tyrone, Chicken Little and the happy couple, Tyrone was wearing a scowl. Not a big deal on its own because a lot of tough guys throw the look as street armor, but Tyrone was eyeballing Cody, and in particular Lindsay Day—always from a vantage point of near anonymity. I studied the photos like a professor grades a thesis. At first it looked like Tyrone disliked Lindsay, but it wasn't that. I'd seen how people behave from a thousand stages when they think they aren't being watched. Tyrone's expressions read lust, frustration and jealousy—he wanted Lindsay for himself—a classic covet. The stalking of the girl proved it. And now the one person who had stood in his way was dead. My phone buzzed three times and slid a foot across my coffee table before I noticed it.

It was a text from Jake. The game was on, and tonight was the night. I guzzled the champagne and nearly choked on the fruit. I gagged twice but held it and convinced myself this was a good omen.

I packed up a few more snacks, mostly nut varieties and water, and got ready to hit the road and sit on Moscow Mule. Before I left, I called Mrs. Wiggins.

"Your voice sounds much stronger, Violet. On the mend then?"

"Not my fighting best but getting there."

"Glad to hear it. Can I get you anything before I head out?"

"I'm all set, Louis, thanks for asking."

"All right then I'll—"

"Got time to update an old lady on your case?"

"I don't know any old ladies, but I'll come and fill *you* in," I said.

"You're silly," she said with a chuckle.

Mrs. Wiggins sipped tea while I filled her in on my findings. When I was finished, she made her slender fingers into a steeple.

"I don't like the *Disruptor* angle one bit, Louis."

"You've heard of them?"

"Old people are wise, Louis, didn't anybody tell you that? Promise me you'll call the law this time. *Disruptors* are some tough hombres!"

"Promise."

She raised a warning eyebrow with a theatrical head tilt.

CHAPTER FORTY-TWO

Jake didn't recognize the number but had a good idea who it was.

"Yeah?"

"You're a hard man to track down, even for me."

"The Trusty Lesbo, I take it," Jake said.

"Is that her? Is it Trusty?" Stephen Bore asked from his spot on the floor. Jake raised a silencing finger toward him, then put his phone on speaker.

"A lot o' firewalls around you, Jake Strickland, but as you can see, I found you."

"What do you want?"

"It was kinda cute how you beat that court case. What I wouldn't have paid to see that cunt lawyer Janie Gilbert's face."

Jake said nothing.

"Anyway, I'm calling to tell you your boy, Crasher, ain't safe."

"From you and the other *Disruptor* losers? You're children in a bouncy castle at best."

"You just made it to my list."

"Flattered," Jake said.

"Trusty, I'm sorry!" Stephen shouted.

"Who the fuck is that?"

"It's your boy Bore. Mission Hills is blown."

"Trusty I—aaaaaaagh!"

Jake cut Bore off by twisting the blade in his hamstring back and forth until he passed out.

"You wanna try his cell to see if it's really him?"

"I recognize his whine. You're a fucking dead man, Strickland."

"Nope, you were, the minute you stepped into Crasher's world."

The line went dead. Jake texted his half-brother then called the local cops and gave them Bore's info and address.

CHAPTER FORTY-THREE

Fifteen minutes after leaving Mrs. Wiggins the ol' gal and I were up the street from the tent gang's minivan, which was parked around the corner from the guesthouse like before. It turns out a stakeout isn't boring when you know something is going to go down. I sat for two hours. Shielding the light with my hand, I checked my phone for the time. The crew should be along in twenty minutes or so. I noticed my battery was so low I could barely see the battery icon. I thought of Mrs. Wiggins and how she'd kill me if I weren't able to call the law because of a dead phone. I took my car charger out of the glove compartment and plugged in the phone. Like clockwork, the three darkly clad women approached the van—not with speed but certainly with purpose. I wondered what it was like being part of the heist team. Did they get nervous? I certainly was. But part of my excitement was because a rock drummer was going to take down the gang that had eluded L.A.'s serve-and-protect boys, and whipped media outlets into a frenzy. I forced myself to keep my ego in check and stay focused—we had a long way to go yet.

The ol' gal had two-thirds of a tank and the oil topped up—she was all set. Once on the freeway, the van held at ten miles an hour above the limit and signaled every lane change without fail. They were nothing more than an innocent group of soccer moms going for a drive...at three a.m. There was the occasional Highway Patrol car, but they let drivers be for the most part. If they saw an accident or obvious drunk driver they'd spring into action, but cars gunning twenty-five over down the six-lane at that hour were given safe passage. It was something I always appreciated as a drummer heading home after a late-night gig. Speeding during the day was a different animal.

The van reduced speed and inched into the slow lane, edging toward the Rosecrans Boulevard exit—the same exit I'd used to get to Trusty's girlfriend's bungalow. My heartbeat ticked up a notch at the thought of Trusty the hellion. Once off the ramp the options were El Segundo, Manhattan Beach, Hermosa Beach and Redondo Beach. We headed west on Rosecrans toward the water. The plan was to follow the crew to the house, park at least a block away and come in on foot. I'd find a good vantage point and seek out the deadly taser girl in the shadows. If I didn't clock her, I'd assume she was perhaps inside, but I knew she'd be at the house. Something told me she was at every robbery. I liked it better when hackers lurked in low-ceiling basements eating junk food and drinking sodas.

We held on Rosecrans for about three miles, which included a half-dozen set of lights. Most of the limited traffic was semi-trucks heading for the airport and ride-share cars. Our trip took us past the massive Chevron plant, which was the size of a tiny city. Giant plumes of white smoke spewed from three separate stacks. The van stopped at Highland Avenue, just two short blocks from the Pacific Ocean. I slowed as much as I could. Being the only other vehicle on the long stretch of road I didn't want to catch up to them. The light finally changed and the van turned left, heading south. At Thirty-third Street, the crew took a slow right turn down near Ocean Drive and parked three spots from a tented mansion. It looked as though the company had had to sew four tents together to cover the beast. I took the alley prior and gunned it to the end of the block. When I emerged from the narrow lane I lucked out and found a spot. I grabbed my phone and was about to hit the pavement when I saw the phone was still dead.

What the...

I double-checked—a useless piece of dead technology. I checked my cigarette lighter. Nothing, the lighter gave no heat. I cursed. The car is in her fifties—what did I expect? I considered driving to the nearest cop shop but I'd need my phone to look up the address, not to mention that the tent gang was usually done in less than fifteen minutes. I left the phone and grabbed a tiny penlight from my glove compartment since my phone was useless. As I was locking up the steering wheel I decided the ride would be fine, but I might not. I secured the club in the locked position and hefted it out with me. If a cop or neighborhood rent-a-cop happened on a two hundred-and-twelve-pound brother sprinting down the alley with a club in his hand I'd have problems, unless I could get my story out—and even then...

Five different dogs protested as I sprinted past their homes. I took cover at the end of the alley behind a lamppost with a cypress hedge growing beside it. The van sat empty. Nothing moved. The soundtrack was waves crashing against Manhattan Beach's shores. Then with the effortless grace of a fox and the soundless steps of a cat, a dark figure hurried to the tented house and quickly disappeared—Trusty!

I thought of Mrs. Wiggins as I broke my promise to her. I was going in because I had no choice. I was about to enter a dark home with three burglars and a psychotic taser-freak, knowing that at least one of them, probably Trusty, was a murderer. To hell with it, this one was for Meredith, Jake, Lindsay Day, and above all, Cody. I figured making it about anybody but me would steel my resolve and push me forward. As I crossed the street I felt as though I were wading waist-deep through the Pacific's waters. I didn't want to go in, but I moved right foot after left and repeated. I squeezed the club in my hand. It felt good, like I had support. It was Eunice the Club and Crasher against the world.

I crept down the side of the house, following Trusty's route. I moved as if I were negotiating a field of landmines. The house and neighboring mansion nearly kissed each other at more than a few points. Manhattan Beach residents build their behemoths on every legal inch of real estate allowed by multiple permits. Halfway down the walk I found a portion of tent flapping in the wind like a loose piece of skin. Checking it out revealed a thin slice from the ground up to about five feet high—tall enough for a short person to slide through—Trusty's entrance. My assumption was that the crew had entered through the back door like they had at Kensington's and the other victims' houses.

I shimmied through the slit and was immediately standing in front of a side door with frosted glass. I tried the handle. It was open. I was lucky the hinges were well-oiled; the door was soundless. I found myself on a landing with a short hallway. I pulled out the tiny penlight, turned it on and held it tight against my thigh. There were stairs on either side of me: up to my right and down to my left. I chose left and descended. The blond hardwood stairs were wide, treaded planks in an open concept. Muted moonlight shone through occasional rips in the tent. The two-and-a-half-inch-thick planks were solid, making no squeak whatsoever—more good luck. Eight steps down took me to a landing, then a right turn. After eight more steps I was on what seemed to be the bottom floor, where the ceiling was at least nine feet tall. I wedged myself into a corner, crouched low and listened. I didn't hear anything but that didn't mean I was alone. After a moment I stood up and crept down a wide hall. Artwork was on both walls, which meant the gang either hadn't picked them yet or felt they had little value.

I entered a room on my left and found it to be an empty bedroom. Back in the hall I took a right for three long strides and entered a second bedroom, also empty. Twelve feet farther down the hall I entered a large game room and bar area. The room had everything a man would need in his cave: giant TV, bar, pool table and so on. It was too dark to tell if anything was missing. Every now and then the moon would cast a shadow over a piece of furniture and freak me out, thinking Trusty was coming for me. I did a quick check behind the bar and was about to make my way up to the next level when I tripped and fell on something that caught my foot. I did a push up and realized it was a body. And I was lying right on top of it—her, in fact. She was short like Trusty, had a pixie haircut and blue-grey eyes that were wide with terror. It was one of the tent gang. I got to a kneeling position and checked for a pulse, already knowing it was too late. I pulled my hand back quickly, startled by the feel of something odd about the neck. I shone my light briefly and touched the other side of her neck. A neck vertebra jutted out grotesquely. Her neck had been broken. The *Disruptor* hacker was cleaning up loose ends.

Damn, that Trusty works fast...

Killing the light, I felt around until I found my steering wheel club and carried on. There were two other rooms on the bottom floor. I checked them with some haste, not expecting to find anyone. Now I was back up on the ground floor, where I had entered. I found a giant great room beyond the up staircase. A shaft of light pierced the room, revealing a massive sectional couch with a chunky-legged coffee table sitting in front of it. I made my way down the hall and stopped in my tracks. To my right it looked as though someone was standing half in and half out of a closet, working inside. It had to be a member of the tent gang, and she had a tiny penlight similar to mine. I had nowhere to go: I'd be exposed as soon as she pulled her head out of the opening. I picked up my pace, moving toward her. The plan was to get behind her and choke her asleep. Then I'd find something to bind her with and use her cell phone to bring in the law. I closed the distance—five feet, four, three and then stopped in my tracks. Something was wrong. The body didn't move, not so much as a hair. The only way to stand that still was to hold your breath, and why would you do that if you're in the middle of burgling a joint? I eased closer and put a hand to the shoulder—nothing. I did it again and gave it a slight tug. The body tilted back toward me and slumped to the floor. The eyes were wide like her partner's on the floor below. I didn't recognize her, which meant Moscow Mule was in another part of the house. This second tent gang member had been propped and partially wedged into the dryer of an industrial-sized, stacked washer-dryer. Her neck was also jacked up, only this time there was a strangulation mark that was thicker than piano wire but thinner than standard rope. I spun around, thinking someone was behind me, but it was nothing. I killed her flashlight and peeled my ears. For all I knew, Trusty was upstairs finishing off Moscow Mule. I rummaged the dead woman's pockets for a cell phone but she wasn't carrying. Maybe that was policy. She was dressed in black from head to toe, with little booties over her dark sneakers: all precautions that had done her little good, thanks to a lone *Disruptor*.

My next option was to back out of the house and knock on doors until someone answered and called the law. Option two was to move upward and face the killer, maybe save Moscow in the bargain, because even though she was a thief, she didn't deserve a fate like her compadres. I killed my light now that my eyes had adjusted, slapped the club in my hand twice for good measure, and moved on. It seemed like a fight or flight situation and smart money said I should fly, but I was taking the stairs one at a time at a clip. Sometimes I think animals are smarter than we are.

When my head reached the top step, I flattened myself on the staircase and peeked over the lip at another great room, this one backed by a giant kitchen. The open-concept room was empty and silent. The bedrooms would all be behind the kitchen somewhere, and that's where Moscow would be—the news reports about the burglaries all mentioned that homeowners lost high-priced shoes, suits, jewelry, electronics, and so on. I wasn't using any stealth as I hustled through the large room and kitchen. I was growing tired of the many hallways in this house. I practically jogged down the bowling-lane-sized run and merely peeked into the rooms as I passed. Wide double doors brought the hallway to an end. Behind their thick, exotic wood, I could barely make out voices . A sneak attack wasn't going to work. I kicked the doors inward and jumped into the room with my club held in both hands just above my waist.

"This shit is over ladies," I said, and flicked on the light.

CHAPTER FORTY-FOUR

Trusty had Moscow backed into a corner between a high wardrobe and the wall. She was approaching with her taser buzzing. She turned slowly with confidence.

"Crasher, I knew you were out there lurking like a bitch, but I didn't think you had the balls to come in here—especially after last time we met."

Her laugh carried a tone a demon would envy. As I sized her up while trying to come up with a cutting remark, Moscow Mule rushed Trusty from behind. It was a solid plan, except that Trusty was a half-step faster than lightning. She wheeled around. Moscow knew she was too slow and tried to recoil but still received a brief zap from the taser.

"Shit," Moscow said, jumping back and shaking out her arm. Trusty laughed mockingly and maneuvered to a position to battle both Moscow and me at the same time. Moscow slid out of the corner and stood opposite Taser Girl. I moved the club side to side in a two-handed grip. Moscow bounced on the balls of her feet, boxer-style—and I was glad of it; it meant my partner knew what she was doing. Trusty feigned a lunge at Moscow but changed course on the head of a pin and threw a back kick at my head. I was on my way in with a low club strike when I was forced to lean way back—Keanu Reeves-style in the Matrix movie—to avoid her foot, which caught the tip of my nose. It stung a little but it was the message that really hurt: this dame can fight! I nearly lost my footing and Trusty copped to it and pursued me. Her taser caught me high on the shoulder. I struggled to knock it away with my club hand and got it there but with no power. The volts coursed through my body. Moscow grabbed Trusty by the hood of her hoodie and hauled her back and around in a dance-like move. Trusty flew into a low dresser, hit the floor and was up in seconds flat. She was incredibly nimble for a plump woman.

I shook my shoulder out and thanked Moscow. "Lou Crasher," I said as Moscow Mule and I stood beside each other breathing heavily.

"Heather Cox, but they call me Moscow Mule." We bumped fists briefly without looking at each other. We didn't dare risk a split-second taking eyes off the lethal weapon in front of us.

Trusty gently placed the taser on the bed, daring us to make a move. With a sadistic grin she removed the hooded sweatshirt and tossed it on the bed. Under the shirt she wore two more sweaters. What I had categorized as fast-moving and heavyset turned out to be dead wrong. Trusty was ninety-six percent muscle and bone. If four percent was fat, you sure could have fooled me. Veins leapt from pale skin and several tattoos dotted the paleness.

"Fuck me," I said, taking in the spectacle.

"Sorry drummer, you're not my type," she smiled.

"Jeeeeezus," Heather whispered. "She doesn't even look real."

Trusty moved her eyes to Heather.

"Now you, girlfriend, are certainly my type. Too bad I don't have time to take that body of yours for a ride."

The two obviously knew each other but Heather seemed as impressed as I by Trusty's physique. My heart was still beating way too fast to continue. Time to stall.

"Let me guess, you've got a dragon tattooed on your back ala Lizbeth Salander."

"That bitch wishes she was me."

Either Heather picked up on my play or she needed more time.

"Tell me one thing, you fucking psycho, why did you kill that kid? We could have taken his ass," Heather said.

"I come and go, kiss and kill as I please. And he needed kill-ing," she paused. "Or not, who gives a shit? What you should be asking is why I killed your pathetic crew members downstairs."

Heather bit her lip and tried to force back tears, but it was no use. After holding Trusty's eyes for almost half a minute she turned to me. I whispered that Trusty was telling the truth.

Heather slowly raised her hands to a boxing position and bent her knees slightly. "Let's kill this cunt, Crasher."

"With fucking pleasure."

We spread out and put Trusty between us. She scooped up the taser almost faster than my eye could track it and buzzed it two quick bursts. Heather told her it wouldn't save her. Trusty kicked an eighteen-inch-high ottoman at me. I hopped over it with ease and moved forward. Trusty faked a jab with her weapon at Heather, then switched to a front kick, which sent Heather stumbling backward. Trusty's next kick came for my mid-section. I blocked it with a downward block with the club. She followed her attack with a short right that caught me on the button. It rocked me. but I kept my feet just long enough for her left-spinning back kick to catch me high on the chest. I crashed through a set of French doors onto a tiny balcony and tumbled over the railing. I did a full flip but managed to grab the bottom iron with my left hand and miraculously maintain a grip on Eunice. If not for the taught tent I'd have flown God-knows-where. I saw the top of Trusty's head come into view. Her grin was intoxicated with hatred and violence. Heather leapt onto her back and began applying a choke from behind.

Atta girl!

The two women staggered back into the master, which gave me time to scramble back over the rail and onto the balcony. As I entered, Trusty judo-flipped Heather onto the floor. She exhaled loudly. I charged, let loose a battle cry and launched a flying sidekick at the enemy. My form wasn't pretty but, aided by my speed, the kick caught her square in the side of the ribs. Trusty flew onto the bed, bounced up high and into the wall. Heather and I wasted no time.

We hurled ourselves on top of her. "Work her torso until she's cashed!" I shouted, remembering what Jake had told me about how two men take on a dangerous single enemy: one up top, one below, and go to work. I grabbed Trusty's muscular legs and wrapped my arms around them in a bearhug. She wasn't going anywhere so long as Heather kept her busy up top, which she did. Out of the corner of my eye I could see Heather land several well-placed blows to Trusty's face. Trusty took them all, kicking and bucking like a mule, but I had her in a lock a gator couldn't escape.

"Keep going Heather. Tune this bi—"

Then I heard the buzzing sound. Heather shook and lost her grip and rolled off. Then I felt the taser on my back. I let go and rolled away. Trusty followed but I rolled onto something hard.

My equalizer...Eunice!

Trusty came in for another zap but was met by a fast-moving club to the shinbone. She went down with an "oomph" sound. Heather was on the floor, apparently out cold. It didn't matter because I was in survival mode, which wasn't far from kill mode. From a kneeling position I brought the club down axe-swing style and cracked Trusty's kneecap to mush. This time she howled. I crawled to her faster than a cockroach does when the light comes on, got behind her and applied a choke.

"Night-night girlfriend," I said, sinking the naked choke deep. All I needed was three to five seconds to cut off the blood supply that flowed through the carotid arteries to her brain and she'd be snoring. Then I'd call the law and be done. But once again I heard my new least-favorite sound: the buzz.

She had somehow managed to get the taser to my forearm. I cried out and convulsed but was determined not to quit. Heart rate: up. Ears: hot and ringing. Time: to kill. My body quivered. Bile was rising. I was going to pass out. Trusty would no doubt kill me at that point. I tried to control my arm. I did one final convulsion and then everything stopped.

The black curtain of sleep came into view, but to my surprise, didn't close. My arms were still locked around Trusty but she was motionless. I unlocked and slid from under her. She was no longer a threat. I rolled over and threw up. I rallied and turned back to Trusty. One look at her neck confirmed it. Somehow during my convulsions my torqueing had snapped her neck. Her *Disruptor* days were over. A fitting end, seeing as what she'd done to the tent gang members—and to Cody. I fell to my back and sucked oxygen in deep. I moved my hands to my groin area. No piss. I was two for two, thank God.

I got to my hands and knees and saw Heather in the same position. She smiled for a moment, then slowly clutched her left arm and fell to her side.

"I don't feel so hot, Crasher," there was fear in her voice.

By the time I crawled to her she was out. Or so I thought. I shook her gently then checked her pulse: nothing.

"No!" I said moving into CPR mode. I put her on her back, pumped the chest, then breathed into her mouth. "Come on girl, you're too young for this shit!"

I don't know how many times I repeated the drill or for how long, but eventually she came back. I didn't know the woman, knew she was a thief, yet still my eyes teared up with relief. It must have had something to do with fighting a common enemy to the death.

"Jesus, you scared me," I said, propping her head on my lap.

"I had heart issues as a, as a kid," her voice was weak.

"I guess the taser didn't help," I smiled.

"That bi—bitch."

"Okay, no more talking. I'm going to use your phone and call the law."

"Wait, you need to know why. Trusty, years ago, she stole my parents' identity."

"Okay, if you insist on talking, let me do most of it, I'll fill in the blanks."

She nodded her head slowly. For the first time I noticed her eyes were turquoise—beautiful.

"Stole your parents' identity and what? Ruined them? They couldn't recover?"

"Yes."

"So why work with her to rob houses?"

"Re— revenge."

I thought about it a moment. "You wanted to get close to her. Gain her trust, pun intended, and then drop the hammer. Is that it?"

She nodded weakly. I thought some more. I had a thousand questions, but I didn't want to keep her talking too long.

"So, you met her how? Don't answer that, doesn't matter. She's a part of a sub-culture group called *Disruptor*; you reach out—she's a hacker what did she hack for—"

"Tented houses. Lo— locations—schedules. Alarm codes."

That added up. "Is it true that Trusty killed the kid, Cody, on her own? You other cats didn't know anything about it?"

She said she didn't know Trusty was in the house but often got a feeling she or something was ghosting them. She went on to squeak out that her parents went so broke they lost their home, the home Heather grew up in. I tried to keep her quiet, but she kept going. I stopped her at one point and called an ambulance and the law.

I felt her pulse and it was weak. She looked pale as well. I pocketed her phone.

"Heather, please, you need to save your strength. Help is on—"

A quiet breath came out and her lids closed. I went back into rescue mode, but she wasn't coming around. I believed her story one hundred and ten percent of the way. I liked her; felt for her and her family. We all know the clichés about revenge and the price that comes with it, but I didn't care, this woman was good. I was shouting her name and pushing on her chest when the first responders came into the room and hauled me aside. Two thick-necked, paunchy cops wrestled me out of the room. A uniform was assigned to "sit on me." It seemed as though the paramedics worked on her for hours but it was probably more like minutes. I flipped through Heather's phone absentmindedly. Every now and again voices called out from different quadrants of the home. They were finding bodies.

Detectives were coming back up the stairs when I noticed a name in Heather's contacts that rocked me—I knew the name and the number. I maintained a poker face and slid the phone back into my pocket. One of the thickly built detectives wanted everyone out. The rules were that nobody except an assigned, uniformed officer was to be in the house until the coroner showed up to announce what we already knew. The tent gang members, including Heather and their hacker, were all dead, which made me the sole survivor. It didn't feel right. I wasn't part of the tent gang or the anti-society group, yet I felt a pang of guilt in my gut that Heather and Cody were dead.

I sat with a detective and ran the whole story down for him. There were a few questions I wouldn't answer, and I threatened to lawyer up when he pushed. We sat up front in his cruiser because I told him, "This brother doesn't sit in the back of cop cars unless under arrest." He bristled at having to clear off some paperwork on the passenger seat. After an hour of our back-and-forth tennis match, I was free to go but would need to swing by the cop shop for a full statement.

I still had Heather's phone in my pocket. Back in my ride I opened the phone and stared at the familiar contact. I began scrolling through her pictures. Maybe she took pics of some of the houses or maybe the stolen gear. There was nothing whatso-ever like that. That made sense seeing as these women used pseudonyms, and the phone I was holding looked a lot like a burner phone. There was one single picture of the tent gang, a selfie. Checking the location and date log it would have been shot back when the crew first got started, three months ago. It could have been the day they sealed their pact or hit their first house. I couldn't take my eyes off one of the members. I wasn't sure why. Then I remembered what her corpse looked like and I shuddered slightly. Still, I gazed at the photo until I understood why I was drawn to her.

Son of a…

I looked at my own dead phone and with a sigh cranked the ol' gal to life and pointed her north toward home.

CHAPTER FORTY-FIVE

The following afternoon I drove by Meredith Billups's home. She seemed the most upbeat since I'd known her..

"Come on in, Mr. Crasher."

I followed her down the hall for what would be my last time. She motioned for me to sit anywhere. I took a spot at the mantle and leaned on it.

"Word is the tent gang are dead, all of them. Is it true?"

"Yes, including the hacker who set them up with the houses—nasty girl, that one."

"Well, it don't bring my son back, but it bring me some kinda peace. I called Jake and thanked him and now I'm thankin' you."

She stood and stuck out a hand. I shook it slowly. It was my cue to leave, but I wasn't done yet.

"You know Cody got that girl, Lindsay Day, pregnant, don't you?"

"That girl was no good."

"What do you mean *was* no good?" I asked.

Her eye lashes batted the slightest bit.

"I meant, I don't know, whatever—"

"Meredith, do you think Lindsay was part of the tent gang?"

For the first time I saw Meredith smile. "I know she was and whatever happened in that house at the beach, she ended up dead. I'm assuming you capped that bitch."

"Three of the crew members were killed by the hacker they called Trusty. When Trusty and I tussled, she ended up dead."

"So, what of it?"

"If you thought Lindsay Day was part of the tent gang, why didn't you let me in on it? I was trying to solve your son's murder, remember?"

She wouldn't meet my gaze, yet she wanted to tell me something. I didn't have the patience to wait her out.

"You said something to someone, or you did something, didn't you? You were working something on your own and were fine with my crawling around in the dark so long as it didn't mess with your gig, right?"

Meredith shifted in her chair and fidgeted with her hands on the tabletop. With a heavy sigh I pulled out Heather's phone and showed her the picture of the tent gang.

"Do you see Lindsay in this photo?" I asked.

"Uh-huh, there she is, that lowdown ho." she said, indicating Boilermaker, aka Shania Simms.

Then I pulled out Cody's phone, the one Meredith didn't know about, and showed her Lindsay Day's actual picture. I held the photos side by side. Meredith blinked, then slowly clutched at her neck area and slumped heavily in her chair.

"They could be twins, couldn't they?" I said pulling the phones away.

Her eyes grew nearly double in size, "Those bitches look—look the same. Are you sure—"

She let it hang and stared far away into a memory.

"Why don't you tell me what you did, Meredith," I said.

She buried her face in her hands for a moment then sat back and spoke with her eyes closed.

"I was coming out of Target and I saw that bitch that trapped my boy. I followed her and watched. I fell asleep but woke to find her leaving her house late. I thought maybe the little ho was going for a booty call. But she ends up in a van with two other dark-clothed people, and they go climbing into a house with a tent on it. Immediately I knew what's goin' on, so I'm 'bout to call the Po-Po when this scary-looking bitch taps on my window—nearly gave me a damn heart attack."

"That would be Trusty, the hacker."

"Uh-huh. She got this taser but doesn't use it on me cause I talk fast—real fast. I tell her why I'm there and then, wouldn't you know, it the dyke-bitch tells me for three grand she can make my problem go away," she took a long pause at this point. Her eyes welled up. "And I believed her." I could barely hear her.

"So you paid her."

"The next day," she nodded. Her head looked too heavy for her neck and shoulders.

I hated this part and felt like a heel for going where I needed to.

"Meredith, the hacker is the one who shot Cody. I'm so sorry."

She collapsed on the floor and wailed. "I kilt my boy! I kilt my baby boy! Please God, no, I paid that bitch! And she kilt my boy!"

I got down on the floor and held her. At some point I unconsciously began to rock her gently back and forth and told her to let it all out. Trusty obviously had known that Boilermaker wasn't Lindsay but it didn't matter; she was doing what *Disuptors* do. Killing Cody probably was to protect the crew from getting busted, which would fit with Heather's story. I'm sure Trusty was simply going to keep Meredith's money like a true *Disruptor*. I planned on explaining to Meredith, sometime in the future, that Trusty did what she did to keep the crew out of stir. But in that moment, we just rocked to and fro on the cold linoleum.

Jake was leaning against the ol' gal when I got outside.

"I saw on the news the other day a *Disruptor* low-life hacker was popped in El Paso. He had some big dude with him, but the big dude was cashed—flat-lined. The hacker talked about a guy, an intruder that kinda fit your description. An anonymous 9-1-1 call tipped the rollers off. Know anything about it?"

"They say El Paso's nice this time o' year."

But that's all he gave me, which actually was enough.

"The last words you had with Heather," he paused. "What was your take on her?"

"She fed me a story of revenge for her parents," I said. "And I believed every word of it. When we fought that psychopath, Heather gave as good as she got, never backing down. She even saved my ass from a nasty fall," I paused a moment, looking back at the memory.

"I'd have been proud to know her, Jake."

Pushing off my ride he hopped into his Dodge Challenger R/T Scat Pack. Four hundred and eighty-five horses roared to life. The window slid down.

"You're right, you woulda been proud to know her. Shame."

When I'd used Heather Cox's phone to call 9-1-1 at the Manhattan Beach house, the lone number in the contacts was Jake's. I didn't bother bringing it up at that point and probably never would. Whatever connection Jake had had with Heather Cox was his business. He'd either tell me about it or not—probably not. I can't say sadness was in Jake's eyes because I'm not sure I'd know what that looked like. But something heavy was there in the depths of his dark eyes. He pulled out from the curb and rumbled down the street barely above a crawl.

EPILOGUE

It had been three days since my encounter with Meredith. I paid my visit to the cop shop in Manhattan Beach and gave them just about everything I had, including the whereabouts of a condo that I believed belonged to the deceased hacker, and passed the test with flying colors: they weren't going to press any charges against me. Jake had a lawyer on standby for me in any case. I sent a text to Shawn Kensington, the wrestling writer, giving him the short version of the tenth house because I didn't want him telling a bunch of wrestlers that I was a shit-prick. He seemed enthused to hear from me—said he'd get me tickets to a show anytime.

I sat behind the work desk on the phone and chopped it up with boss Big Eddie Carruthers. He seemed happy with our arrangement with me as manager. He even credited me with turning Susie around.

"It seems you got her to ease off the sauce and put in some good work around the Joint. Maybe you should add counseling to your list of talents."

"Hell no, Big Eddie, unless there's a salary bump to it."

"Fat chance!" His big laughed boomed through the earpiece until he disconnected the call. I put the phone down, leaned back in the chair, and closed my eyes. Distant footsteps drew closer. A woman's or small man's—child, maybe. Crasher, always sleuthing. I opened my eyes as she came into the office. Tracy Sanderson's sheepish smile gave me slight satisfaction. I let her go first since it was her party.

"I fucked up and I'm sorry. You were right. Bobby's a fucking moron—wipe that grin off your face, I know you warned me." She stepped into the room and stood over the desk. "Do you know that idiot got drunk at our first gig and tried to get handsy with me on stage? Fucking stage, Lou!"

I kept up the I-tried-to-warn-you face but said nothing.

"I want my drummer back, Lou."

"You get a gig, let me know. I'm back being a gun for hire. And for you, Crasher's price has gone up."

"Did you just fucking third-person me?"

"Crasher does that sometimes," I smiled. She returned the smile.

"Okay. I deserve it. We can talk about the pay raise." She sat down on the edge of the desk. "Are you sure you won't come back full-time?"

I shook my head no. We held a long look. I wondered if we'd ever fire up our friends-with-benefits deal. I think she was wondering as well. She hopped behind the desk, gave me a kiss on the cheek, then clipped down the hall. I closed my eyes again and got a two-minute snooze before a throat-clearing stirred me. I opened my eyes, expecting to see Tracy, but it wasn't her.

"Oh, wow—Nima, my favorite tattoo artist," I said, getting up. "To what do I owe the pleasure?"

"I may have a job for you. That is, if you're still in the P.I. business," she said, looking around the office.

"I am in the P.I. business. This is a side gig to my side gig. What have ya got?"

"I thought maybe you could buy me a drink this time while I tell you about it."

"Happy to," I said, getting up from my chair. "Ya know, I've been doing that chilled tumbler thing."

"Oh?" she said looking around the office. "I don't see a fridge."

"Not here," I said. "My home."
"Home, huh?" she grinned.
"Yes," I nodded.
"Home it is. Mind if I ride with you?"

ACKNOWLEDGMENTS

Right off the top I need to thank my wife Sonia. Thank you for your unconditional love, support and in particular, patience. Ismael Tavera, thanks for your police and ordinance expertise and for your continued friendship. (BTW when we do the ride along I'm riding up front, not in the back pal!). Thanks to all of you who not only pick up my books but read the books of my fellow writers.

JONATHAN J. BROWN is the author of *A Boxing Trainer's Journey: A Novel Based of the Life of Angelo Dundee* and the novella *Moose's Law: A Doug "Moose" McCrae Story* about an ex-football-playing bouncer and "fixer" living in Los Angeles. Brown has also written short stories that have appeared in *Out of the Gutter Online* and in two Palos Verdes library anthologies. In addition, he has written, recorded and performed an audio children's book, *KANU: A Boy's Journey*. His second book in the Lou Crasher series drops in 2020 from Down & Out Books. He currently teaches drums and is a personal trainer. He and his wife enjoy sunny-living in Los Angeles.

JonathanBrownWriter.com